The Bhagavad Gita

BY KEITH HILL

CLASSICS OF WORLD MYSTICISM

Interpretations of Desire:
Mystical love poems by the Sufi master Ibn 'Arabi
I Cannot Live Without You:
Selected poetry of Mirabai and Kabir
Psalms of Exile and Return:
A journey in search of inner healing and unity
The Bhagavad Gita: A new poetic translation

POETRY

The Ecstasy of Cabeza de Vaca
The Lounging Lizard Poet of the Floating World

FICTION

Puck of the Starways
Blue Kisses

NON-FICTION

The New Mysticism
The God Revolution
Striving To Be Human
Experimental Spirituality
Practical Spirituality
Psychological Spirituality

The Bhagavad Gita

A new poetic translation

Keith Hill

attar‖books

Published in 2021 by Attar Books
Auckland, New Zealand

Paperback ISBN 978-0-9951333-7-2
Ebook ISBN 978-0-9951333-8-9
Hardcover ISBN 978-0-9951333-9-6

Copyright © Keith Hill 2021

Keith Hill's right to be identified as author of this work is asserted in accordance with Section 96 of the Copyright Act 1996.

All rights reserved. Except for fair dealing or brief passages quoted in a newspaper, magazine, radio, television or internet review, no part of this book may be reproduced in any form or by any means, or in any form of binding or cover other than that in which it is published, without permission in writing from the Publisher. This same condition is imposed on any subsequent purchaser.

Cover image: Shutterstock

Attar Books is a New Zealand publisher which focuses on work that explores today's spiritual experiences, culture, concepts and practices. For more information visit our website:

www.attarbooks.com

Dedicated to Shri Mauniji Maharaj
whose insights I had the privilege to share
and whose experience and knowledge
brought this translation of
the Bhagavad Gita into the world.

Contents

Preface   9

The Bhagavad Gita

1. The Dejection of Arjuna   17
2. The Yoga of Knowledge   22
3. The Yoga of Action   29
4. The Yoga of Knowledge, Action and Renunciation   33
5. The Yoga of Sacrifice   37
6. Steadfast, Concentrated Meditation on Atman   40
7. Knowledge of the Manifest and Unmanifest   45
8. The Yoga of Brahman   48
9. The King of Sciences and the King of Secrets   51
10. The Yoga of Supernal Qualities   55
11. The Vision of the Cosmic Form   59
12. The Yoga of Devotion   66
13. Distinguishing Between Field and Knower of the Field   69
14. Identifying the Three Guna's Qualities   73
15. The Yoga of Purushottama   76
16. Distinguishing Between Divine and Demonic Natures   79
17. Identifying the Three Qualities of Faith   82
18. The Yoga of Liberation Through Renunciation   85

Appendices

The philosophic background   95
Notes on discourses   105
Glossary of Indian words   155
To the reader   158

Preface

Two armies face each other, seconds away from mutual annihilation. Between them is parked a chariot. In the chariot are the renowned warrior, Arjuna, and his divine charioteer, Krishna. Having surveyed the two armies, and recognised that his kinsmen are ranged on both sides, Arjuna sinks onto the chariot's floor, so overcome with grief at the thought of the forthcoming slaughter and his role in it that he is unable to stand, let alone take up his bow and fight. Krishna looks down at his friend, then utters these indelible words:

> You grieve for those who require no grief,
> justifying yourself with false words of wisdom:
> wise men mourn neither living nor dead.
> For there was never a time when I was not,
> nor when you nor these kings did not exist,
> nor, hereafter, when we will cease to be.

In a few words the dramatic scenario of a doubting warrior is lifted from narrative poetry into the rarer reaches of mystical philosophy. Thus begins arguably the most eloquent disquisition on the immortality of the spiritual self in all world literature.

The *Bhagavad Gita* has been described as the jewel in the crown of the *Mahabharata*, the work in which it is embedded. The *Mahabharata* is fifteen times the length of the New Testament. It narrates the adventures of the five Pandu brothers, describing their exotic encounters with courtesans, villains, magicians, supernaturally-empowered men and women, and demi-gods and gods.

Set against this colourful background, the *Bhagavad Gita* is a tranquil pool, summarising the essence of Indian spirituality.

In eighteen discourses it presents an analysis of the nature of the self, of the cosmos and of the Divine, and maps the paths by which the self may disentangle itself from material existence, gain knowledge, and progress towards God-realisation. It is due to the way it explores humanity's spiritual possibilities that the *Bhagavad Gita* is considered not just the greatest of India's spiritual treatises, but one of the most profound texts in all world literature.

Precisely when the *Bhagavad Gita* was written is not known. Scholars agree it was likely written between the fifth and second centuries BCE. This places its composition during what has been termed the Axial Age, a period when a significant shift in spiritual outlooks occurred, when Gautama Buddha conceived his teaching, Pythagoras introduced philosophy to the Greeks, the Chinese sage Lao Tzu developed the concept of the Dao, and Indian meditators wrote the *Upanishads*.

The *Bhagavad Gita* made a powerful addition to this innovative period, contributing to the Axial era's shift from mythological thought towards more abstract ways of conceiving our spiritual connection to reality. The traces of this shift remain visible in the layers of the text, with numerous mythological figures identified alongside abstract philosophic ideas. Key to the latter is Brahman, in which God is conceived in transcendent terms. The poem also presents Krishna as a personalized form of that abstract God.

Who wrote the *Bhagavad Gita* is also not known. The *Mahabharata*'s authorship is traditionally ascribed to Vyasa, the poet-sage named in the *Bhagavad Gita.*, who is also said to be the author of the *Brahma Sutras*. It is possible Vyasa wrote the original text of the *Bhagavad Gita*, but as we know nothing about him except his name this remains conjectural. Where scholars are agreed is that the text we now possess is likely to have been written by various hands. Of the eighteen discourses, the earliest echo the language and thought of the *Upanishads* and Sankhya philosophy. The concepts of an entirely abstract God named Brahman, of purusha (spirit) and prakriti (matter), and of the gunas (the three fundamental tendencies of matter) date to before 200 BCE. One scholarly theory is that around this time a group who viewed Krishna as the embodiment of the divine may have added the emphasis on Krishna that runs through the poem. However, the artful weaving of the impersonal and personal aspects of deity through the poem mean it is difficult to make definitive statements regarding when and how it was composed.

Each discourse ends with colophon that describes the *Bhagavad Gita* as an *Upanishad*. In a literary sense, the *Upanishads* are those books in the *Vedas* (the oldest Indian spiritual writings) which expound the Indian spiritual philosophy and practice. Thus, the *Bhagavad Gita* may be considered the *Upanishad* of the *Mahabharata*. The title of each discourse varies between editions. Those used here were selected by Shri Muniji Maharaj.

This version of the *Bhagavad Gita* was completed in 1991, at the instigation of Shri Muniji Maharaj, during a three-month period I spent on his ashram in Rajasthan. I must admit that when Shri Muniji first suggested I create a new poetic version I was not convinced there was any need for it, as there already existed innumerable versions in English. I couldn't see the point in adding another. However, Shri Muniji was adamant. At that time the only poetic version was Sir Matthew Arnold's translation into Victorian verse, and the combined prose and verse version by Christopher Isherwood and Swami Prabhavananda. My aim accordingly became to create a version accessible to modern readers that avoided the stilted Victorianisms of Arnold's translation, and offered a complete version of the text in poetry. In 2008 I revised the text to make it more readable and added the glossary and notes. Since then a number of poetic versions have been published, each with different aims. Most notable are Stephen Mitchell's edited response to the text, and Barbara Stoller Miller's more accurate , who sought

I am not a Sanskrit scholar. Accordingly, Shri Muniji proposed that as a basic translation I use the literal word-for-word English transliteration provided by the staff of Kalyama-Kalpataru for Jayadayal Goyandka's *Srimad Bhagavadgita*, published by Gita Press. To provide background knowledge, Shri Muniji gave me a copy of *The Gospel of Selfless Action*. This is a translation into English of Mahatma Gandhi's Gujarati version of the *Bhagavad Gita*, carried out by Gandhi's secretary, Mahadev Desai. Desai's notes were particularly useful to me, as they provide extensive background information, draw attention to key philosophic and spiritual concepts, and offer an ethical and philosophic context for readers approaching the poem from a Western perspective. Of course, many other translators also offer these contextual materials.

When writing a new version of an ancient poem, a central question is what style to use. I wanted the language to be precise, in order to convey the philosophic concepts as exactly as possible. I also wanted to convey a sense that the poem is a dramatic as well as philosophic dialogue, spoken on the cusp of war. I felt a degree of formality was required to achieve this balance. This meant free verse was not appropriate, while any rhyme scheme would require frequently disrupting the sense in order to fit words into a poetic pattern. I accordingly chose blank verse. It has been established since Elizabethan times as a powerful medium for writing dramatic dialogue, which is the *Bhagavad Gita's* literary genre. Avoiding a set stanza length also allowed the length of individual verses to be varied to fit what is being said. My aim is that the style of this version allows for an accurate reflection of the *Bhagavad Gita's* philosophic concepts while also conjuring something of its poetic power and majesty.

As I worked through the word-for-word transliteration, Shri Muniji suggested alternative English words wherever he considered a word I had selected was inconsistent with his knowledge of Sanskrit and his understanding as a yogic practitioner. I soon realised that it was necessary to leave a significant number of Sanskrit words untranslated. I did this first in the interests of intellectual precision. The Sanskrit text has many technical words for which there is no exact equivalent in English. It is also useful for readers to be reminded that much in this poem is foreign and unfamiliar: it was written 2,500 years old, and its conceptual outlook is naturally very different from our modern worldview.

As a result, there will certainly be many words, concepts and statements that on first reading make little sense. To help, I have provided a glossary to elucidate all Sanskrit terms, while notes explain the Indian mythological, religious and cultural references. Numerous extensive commentaries have been written on the *Bhagavad Gita*. My notes make no claim to be either exhaustive or authoritative; they are designed to elucidate the key characters and concepts that lie behind the text. In the notes on each discourse I have occasionally included my own response as a reader, but because my intention is to provide clarity for readers I have avoided offering my own interpretations. Many interpretations are available elsewhere. For the rest, if parts of the text remain mysterious—poetry naturally challenges us that way.

The *Bhagavad Gita* needs to be read in the context of its place in the *Mahabharata*. The following summarises the principal events that culminated in a civil war, on the brink of which the *Bhagavad Gita* is set.

There were once two princely brothers named Dhritarastra and Pandu. On the death of their father, the crown was supposed to be passed on to Dhritarastra, the eldest, but as he was blind Pandu became king instead. When Pandu died the crown was then passed to his eldest son, Yudhishthira. But Dhritarastra's eldest son, Duryodhana, found this unsatisfactory. Believing he was the rightful heir, he arranged a dice game by which he cheated Yudhishthira not only of his kingdom but of everything he and his brothers possessed. Naturally, the Pandu brothers—Arjuna amongst them—were upset at this, especially as Duryodhana had used supernatural means to ensure he won. After a period of argument Duryodhana struck a deal. The Pandus were to go into exile for twelve years, then hide incognito in the kingdom for one year more. During this time Duryodhana would rule. If, at the end of the thirteen years, the Pandus remained undetected, Duryodhana would surrender the crown and the Pandus would rule.

After many adventures, the Pandus successfully completed the task. But when they demanded the return of the kingdom,

Duryodhana, having acquired a taste for kingship, refused to surrender it. The Pandus consulted, decided their position was righteous, and declared war on Duryodhana and their other kinsmen, the sons of Dhritarastra.

With war inevitable, both Arjuna and Duryodhana approached Krishna, seeking his support. Duryodhana arrived first, and finding Krishna asleep, sat on a chair and waited. Arjuna arrived shortly after and took up a position of supplication at the foot of the bed. When Krishna awoke he thus saw Arjuna first.

The crisis was explained to Krishna, each imploring Krishna to take his side in the forthcoming conflict. Being related to both, Krishna said he would assist both sides. To one he would offer the services of his army, to the other himself, although he personally would not fight. As he had seen Arjuna first on waking, he gave Arjuna first choice. Arjuna chose Krishna, to have his wisdom to draw on during the conflict. Duryodhana was also pleased, as he had Krishna's large army.

The first day of the war arrived. Seated in his palace, the blind King Dhritarastra asked his minister, Sanjaya, what was happening. The sage Vyasa had offered to use his magical powers to restore Dhritarastra's sight for the duration of the battle, that he might witness it all himself. Not wishing to see the slaughter, Dhritarastra declined. Vyasa then gave Sanjaya magic sight so he could not only see what happened but also penetrate the hearts and minds of every participant, enabling him to recount to Dhritarastra everything thought, felt and done.

Thus we come to the moment at which the *Bhagavad Gita* begins. Alone in his palace with Sanjaya, Dhritarastra asks what is happening on the battlefield. It is on the wings of Sanjaya's response that the *Bhagavad Gita* soars.

The Bhagavad Gita

Discourse One

Dhritarastra commanded:
1. Report, Sanjaya. How fare my children,
and great King Pandu's sons, together massed
for war on the sacred soil of Kuru?

Sanjaya replied:
2. King Duryodhana, your eldest, his eyes
having appraised the Pandus' armied might,
turned to his great teacher, Drona, saying,
3. "Behold, Master, the massed force of Pandu's sons
set now for combat by your wise disciple,
Dhirstadyumna, wily Drupada's son.
4. Not just Arjuna and Bhima, but scores
of skilful bowmen, as virile in arms
as this famed pair, stand readied to engage us:
Satyaki, Virata, the maharatha
5. Drupada himself, strong Dhrishtaketu,
Chekitana, the valiant Kasiraja,
Purujit, and Saibya, greatest of men,
6. there Yudhamanyu and Uttamaujas,
there Subhadra and Arjuna's brave son,
and here, in close support, the Pandus' sons
by Draupadi, maharatha all five.
7. So stand our enemies, best of Brahmans.
Yet with our distinguished captains we rank
as strong, and own as many worth naming.
8. First your noble self, then Bhishma, Karna,
and Kripa, ever a victor in war,
as too are Ashwatthama, Bhurishrava,

9   and Vikana; plus many heroes more,
        each skilfully wielding weapons of death,
        and each pledged to lay down his life for me.

10   This our force, by Bhishma led, stands too vast
        for defeat; theirs, at Bhima's command,
        while strong, shall prove all too conquerable.

11   Therefore, you men, each hold your position;
        but guard Bhishma, for then will come no surprise."

12   Next, Bhishma, great-uncle to the Kuru's race,
        to assure Duryodhana, erupted
        in a lion's roar, and blew his mighty conch.

13   Drums, cymbals, trumpets, conches and tabors
        joined eagerly in tumultuous noise.

14   At this, Shri Krishna and Arjuna, astride
        their gold chariot yoked to divine white horses,
        both blew on their celestial conches:

15   Shri Krishna's named Panchajanya, Arjuna's
        Devadatta, while wolf-bellied Bhima,
        of terrible deeds, lifted his, Paundra.

16   The three Pandus remaining—Nakula,
        Sahadeva and King Yudhishthira—
        then lifted their conches to their lips;

17   as too Kasiraja the archer, Shikhandhi,
        Dirstadyumna, Virata and Satyaki,
        (called unconquerable by friend and foe),

18   Drupada, the five sons of Draupadi,
        and Subhadra's strong-armed son—all of these,
        great King, lifted their own conches and blew.

19   So terribly that wind-borne sound from earth
        to heaven echoed, it quaked even
        the capacious hearts of your brave sons!

20   This done, Lord of the Earth, and seeing
        your sons arrayed with flights of arrows readied,
        resourceful Arjuna, with Hanuman,
        his bannered ape, chattering in the breeze,

21   took up his bow and said to Shri Krishna,

22 "Rouse the horses, Achyuta, that you may place
my chariot between both armies,
and keep it there so I may clearly see
these warriors now champing for combat,
and who it is I must engage in war.
23 I wish to know what type of men are these
who have prepared for battle to defend
the perverse desires of Duryodhana."
24 Commanded thus by Arjuna, noble king,
Shri Krishna drove the famous chariot
25 between both armies, reined in before Bhishma,
Drona and the assembled kings, and said,
"Perceive, Arjuna, the Kurus all before you now."
26 Arjuna surveyed. His dark eyes beheld,
in both armies ranged, uncles, great uncles,
27 great great uncles, teachers, brothers, sons,
nephews, cousins, comrades, fathers-in-law,
28 and friends. Confronted thus, he then uttered
these words in deep, compassionate sadness.

Arjuna said:
I look upon my kinsmen gathered here for war,
29 and my mouth dries; Krishna, my limbs quail,
my body shudders, hair bristles on my skull.
30 The great bow, Gandiva, slips from my hand;
my skin burns; my mind reels so I cannot stand.
31 I feel such evil forebodings, Krishna,
for I see no good in slaying my kin.
32 I seek no victory, nor a kingdom's crown,
nor even earthly pleasures; for, Govinda,
what use are power, pleasures or life itself,
33 when those for whom we crave that crown, pleasure,
luxury, have themselves renounced both life
and wealth, and are arrayed here now to die?
34 Teachers, nephews, uncles, fathers-in-law,
brothers-in-law and all my kinsmen else,

35 I cannot kill, Krishna, though they would kill me,
   not even to mount the three world's throne,
   much less to claim a paltry earthly crown.
36 What pleasure could derive from slaughtering
   these sons of Dhritarastra, Krishna?
   Sin surely will grip us, usurpers though they be.
37 It cannot, then, behove us to kill them,
   for no happiness follows on killing our kin.
38 And even if they, minds blunted by greed,
   would see no evil in destroying their race,
   nor perceive no sin in treachery to friends,
39 yet how cannot we, who clearly see the sin,
   do otherwise, Krishna, than turn from this crime?
40 For destroy the family, age-old virtues die,
   and virtue lost, vice consumes that family.
41 When vice prevails, Krishna, each family's
   women become corrupt; with their corruption
   society's castes become intermixed.
42 Their bloods thus mixed, both race and race-slayer
   are dragged into hell; deprived of their offerings,
   their deceased ancestors must decline too.
43 Such evils result in intermixed castes;
   then age-old caste and family traditions die,
44 and those for whom family traditions are lost,
   are each assured of residence in hell—
   so, Krishna, our traditions proclaim.
45 What waste! That we, with our intelligence,
   are settled on sin, and from lust for the joy
   which sovereign power devolves are now
   all prepared to annihilate our kin!
46 Krishna, no! Far happier would I be
   if Dhritarastra's sons, weapons in hand,
   killed me in war, unresisting and unarmed.

Sanjaya concluded:
47 So spoke Arjuna on the field of battle;

and casting aside both arrows and bow,
in grief he sank to his chariot's rear.

Thus, in the converse between Shri Krishna and Arjuna, on the science of Yoga, part of the knowledge of Brahman, as sung by the Lord in the Upanishad called Bhagavad Gita, ends the first discourse entitled: The Yoga of the Dejection of Arjuna.

Discourse 2

Sanjaya continued:
1   Then to Arjuna—sunk deep in sorrow,
    heart awash, dark eyes with tears glazed—
    Shri Krishna pronounced these words:

The Lord said:
2   How, at this imperilled time, have such strange
    delusions engulfed you, which noble men
    should shun, and lead to neither heaven nor fame?
3   Do not succumb to unmanliness, Arjuna.
    It is dishonourable. Scorcher of enemies,
    shake off this lowly faint-heartedness. Stand!

Arjuna responded:
4   Tell me, Krishna, how can I, with bow readied,
    arrow cocked, kill both Bhishma and Drona,
    who rather deserve my reverence than death?
5   Surely, I should rather live by begging than slay
    these noble elders, for after their deaths
    all my pleasures will be stained with blood.
6   I am blind. I cannot see which act is preferred:
    to conquer them, or have them conquer us.
    And Dhritarastra's sons, whom if we killed
    I could no longer live, stand before us now!
7   My being is paralysed with faint-heartedness.
    My mind gnaws at duty. I implore you.
    I am your disciple, placed in your hands.
    Tell me how to act, and where my good resides.
8   For if I won an earthly kingdom and wealth,

or even obtained dominion of the gods,
yet still I know I would suffer this grief
which numbs me and desiccates my senses.

Sanjaya said:

9 Thus spoke Arjuna to Shri Krishna, great King,
and with a last, "I will not fight!" fell silent.
10 Then, great Dhritarastra, between both armies,
as if to mock the anguished Arjuna,
Shri Krishna spoke the following words.

The Lord said:

11 You grieve for those who require no grief,
confusing yourself with words of false wisdom;
wise men mourn neither living nor dead.
12 For there was never a time when I was not,
nor when you and these kings did not exist,
nor, hereafter, when we will cease to be.
13 The embodied passes from infancy to death,
just so it enters another body;
the wise are not deceived over this.
14 Heat and cold, pleasure and pain, each arise
when the senses and their objects meet.
But they are transitory. Transcend them, therefore.
15 That man to whom pain and pleasure are the same,
who, Arjuna, by these remains undisturbed,
becomes a candidate for immortality.
16 Nothing can come to be from non-being,
nor can what has existence cease to be;
this reality is perceived by those who know.
17 Understand, that which extends throughout
the entire cosmos is imperishable;
indestructible, none can destroy it.
18 The embodied is immeasurable,
eternal, imperishable; its bodies
finite only. Therefore, Arjuna, fight!

19   Ignorance grips both he who thinks this kills,
     and he who believes this to be killed;
     for, in truth, this neither kills nor is killed.
20   This is not born, nor can it die,
     nor does it only become after birth.
     Unborn, eternal, everlasting and ancient,
     when the body is destroyed, it is not slain.
21   Arjuna, who knows this to be unborn,
     imperishable, immutable and eternal,
     how and whom can he possibly slay?
     How and whom will he cause to be slain?
22   As we discard our worn out garments
     to take up fresh clothes, so the embodied
     discards worn out bodies and enters others new.
23   This, no weapons wound; this, no fire burns;
     water cannot wet it, nor winds dry it.
24   It cannot be cut, burnt, wet or dried out;
     it is eternal, omnipresent, constant,
     immovable and everlasting.
25   Imperceptible by the senses, to the mind
     inconceivable, it is called unchanging.
     Knowing this, you therefore should not grieve.
26   And, Arjuna, even if you think it is always
     being born or dying, your grief is still misplaced.
27   Because death is certain for all who are born,
     and birth assured for those who die—
     and for the inevitable, you should not grieve.
28   Before birth all beings are unknown,
     and at death become unknowable again;
     they are known only between birth and death.
     So what reason do you have to lament?
29   How many perceive the marvel which is this?
     Who speaks of or hears the marvellous in this?
     Yet how many know it even on learning this?
30   This cannot be slain which in any body dwells;
     therefore, Arjuna, it is futile to mourn.

31 But your duty, too, must not be reneged,
as righteous war for the warrior caste is good.

32 Happy those warriors to whom unbidden war comes,
for heaven's gates are thrown open to them.

33 But shirk this righteous war, your honour is lost,
your duty failed, and sin incurred for sure.

34 Worse, the world will tell your disgrace forever,
(for a well-famed man, death would be preferred),

35 and the maharathas who now think you great
will each despise you, thinking fear made you quit;

36 while those who hate you will disparage your deeds,
their words nothing but derision of you.
What could be more disturbing than this?

37 Die, and you gain heaven; a victor, the earth.
Stand then, Arjuna, determined to fight!

38 Viewing alike pain and pleasure, loss and gain,
victory and defeat, prepare for this war.
For in so doing, you will not incur sin.

39 Thus, I have revealed the yoga of jnana.
Hear from me now the yoga of karma;
resorting to which you may shrug action's bonds.

40 On this path no effort can be wasted,
nor can there be divergent result;
even little practice delivers you from fear.

41 In this, Arjuna, the intellect is one-pointed;
thoughts born without aim wander everywhere.

42 Arjuna, the ignorant delight in
the Vedas' letter, claiming none else exists.

43 Driven by desire, heaven is their goal;
their elaborate words merely describe
rituals of many kinds, performed for power
and pleasure, which have rebirth as their fruit.

44 Attached as they are to power and pleasure,
their minds, by such words, are carried far away.
They lack a determined intellect
through which the supreme goal is attained.

45 The three gunas are the Vedas' domain.
Transcend them, Arjuna, and the opposites too,
by thinking clearly, self-controlled and non-attached.

46 As a shallow well has no function when floods
pour in from every side, so that Brahman
who knows has no need for the Vedas' words.

47 Make action your realm, not action's fruit.
Do not let desire for rewards drive your actions;
yet neither become attached to inactivity.

48 Rather, renounce attachment. Practising yoga,
be even-minded in failure and success,
for equanimity is yoga itself.

49 Action is inferior to disciplined action;
seek refuge, therefore, in detachment of mind.
Wretched are they whose motive is the fruit.

50 The disciplined transcend good and evil acts,
so prepare yourself to practise this yoga,
for yoga consists of acting with wisdom.

51 Know that the wise, practising detachment
and renouncing action's fruit, are released
from birth's chains and attain the blissful state.

52 When your mind traverses delusion's morass,
you will become indifferent to voices
which pronounce on either the future or past.

53 When your intellect, not diverted by such words,
at last rests in steadfast concentration,
then you will achieve the practice of yoga.

Arjuna asked:

54 Krishna, how are the wise distinguished
whose minds in samadhi are firmly fixed?
How do those stable-minded speak, sit and move?

Shri Krishna replied:

55 Arjuna, he who rejects the mind's cravings,
and in atman alone finds satisfaction,

he is said to be established in wisdom.

56 Whose mind amid sorrows remains undisturbed,
whose longings for pleasure no longer exist,
who is free of fear, passion and anger,
that sage may be called established in wisdom.

57 He who lives this life devoid of attachment,
who good and evil neither joys in nor resents,
his knowledge is built on a sound foundation.

58 When, as the tortoise withdraws all its limbs,
so he withdraws the senses from their objects,
his knowledge is built on a sound foundation.

59 When the senses are starved, their objects disappear;
taste for them goes too when the Supreme is perceived.

60 For the senses are so rowdy they would
carry away even the wise seeker's mind.

61 With all these in check, the seeker should sit,
focused on me, his senses controlled;
that one may be called established in wisdom.

62 Brood on sense objects, attachments arise;
from attachments come desire; from desire, anger.

63 From anger springs bewilderment;
bewilderment breeds a memory confused;
from memory confused comes lack of reason;
and reason lacking leads to total destruction.

64 But the disciplined seeker, self well-controlled,
unaffected by craving or loathing,
among sense objects tranquilly moves.

65 Stable, serene, his sorrows all cease;
intellect withdrawn, his knowledge is secure.

66 But he whose intellect has no focus
neither understands nor seeks right knowledge;
right knowledge lacking, he has no inner peace;
and without inner peace, how can happiness be?

67 As wind bears away a boat on the water,
so must his discrimination be lost
whose mind is attached to the senses' objects.

68 Therefore, strong-armed prince, the knowledge
of he whose senses are restrained from
all sense objects is built on a sound foundation.
69 When it is night for all other beings,
the disciplined seeker is awake; what keeps
other beings awake, to that seer is night.
70 As rivers drain into the brimming ocean
yet leave the ocean undisturbed,
so the serene are not disturbed by desires,
unlike those who are brimming with wants.
71 That one achieves serenity who
renounces all desires, acts without craving,
and is free of ego and all sense of possession.
72 Arjuna, this is the state of Brahmanic oneness;
established in this, one conquers delusion.
And, at even the moment death strikes,
those who achieve it enter Brahman-nirvana.

Thus, in the dialogue between Shri Krishna and Arjuna, on the science of Yoga, part of the knowledge of Brahman, as sung by the Lord in the Upanishad called Bhagavad Gita, ends the second discourse entitled: The Yoga of Knowledge.

Discourse 3

Arjuna asked:
1. Detached knowledge is superior to action;
such thinking, Krishna, you seem to expound.
So why urge me engage in dread action?
2. Perplexing concepts have confused my mind.
In definite terms please explain, therefore,
that by which the highest good is attained.

Shri Krishna replied:
3. In times past, sinless one, I have taught two paths:
to sankhyas jnanayoga, the path of knowledge;
and to yogis karmayoga, action's path.
4. Who in action refuses to engage
obtains no freedom from action; nor is he
perfected in knowledge who merely ceases to act.
5. Because none is inactive for even a moment;
we are driven to act by prakriti's gunas.
6. Who outwardly curbs his organs of action,
but lets his mind brood on sensual objects,
is lost in delusion and called a hypocrite.
7. But he who controls the senses with his mind
and non-attached, in karmayoga
engages his organs, that man excels.
8. Perform your allotted duty, therefore,
for such action is superior to inaction;
with inaction, not even the body's maintained.
9. Humanity is bound by all action
save that action performed as sacrifice.
So act, Arjuna, free of attachment.

10 The Creator made humanity and sacrifice,
saying, "You only will prosper by this;
may it prove to be the answer to all desires.
11 Cherish the gods with sacrifice and the gods
will cherish you; each other cherished,
know the highest good will be attained.
12 For when so cherished, the gods will grant all
you desire." But he is a thief who takes
the gods' gifts and offers nothing back to them.
13 The virtuous are absolved of their sins
by eating what remains after sacrifice;
those who cook only for the body eat sin.
14 All beings spring from food; food is from rain;
that rain from sacrifice ensues;
and all sacrifice results from action.
15 Know action manifests from prakriti,
and prakriti from imperishable Brahman.
In all sacrifice, therefore, Brahman is present.
16 Who does not keep the wheel turning, Arjuna,
which thus rolls through this world,
sinful, sense-sated, lives his life in vain.
17 But he who in atman alone delights,
who with atman is completely content,
and in atman finds full satisfaction,
such a one has no action to perform.
18 He, in this world, has no bias for things done,
nor yet for whatever remains undone;
no self-interest keeps him dependent on any.
19 So without attachment perform your duty,
for non-attached action leads to the Supreme.
20 Sages like Janaka reached perfection through action;
just maintain the world, whatever you do.
21 For what the great do, so other men do too;
what standard they set, humanity follows.
22 In the three worlds is nothing I need do,
nothing worth having I do not possess—

yet, son of Partha, I continue to act.
23 Should I become weary and cease to act,
all men, Arjuna, would follow my course.
24 If I ceased to act, these worlds would perish;
chaos I would cause, and people's destruction.
25 Just as the unwise act with total attachment,
so the wise should act too, but be non-attached
and mindful always to maintain the world.
26 The knowing should not upset the minds
of the ignorant attached to action; just do
their own duty, and support them in theirs.
27 All action is performed by the prakriti's gunas;
deluded by ego, man thinks, "I am doing this."
28 But he, Arjuna, who well understands
the truth of the gunas and their actions,
perceives that the gunas on the gunas act,
and therefore, remains non-attached.
29 Deceived by prakriti's gunas
men become attached to those gunas' actions;
the wise should not unsettle ignorant minds.
30 So surrendering all your actions to me,
mind concentrated on atman within,
renouncing all fruit and sense of possession,
shake off your fear, Arjuna, and fight!
31 Know those faithful men who, uncomplaining,
always act from this teaching of mine,
achieve release from action's bonds.
32 While those carpers who reject my teaching
live deluded and unknowing—they are all lost.
33 Each living creature follows its nature;
the wise man, too, acts according to his.
How, therefore, could constraint succeed?
34 Likes and dislikes are rooted in sense objects.
Know they ensnare, and refuse their call.
35 Better perform one's own duty, however humble,
than do another's, though well-performed;

better to die fulfilling one's own duty,
for another's contains great jeopardy.

Arjuna inquired:
36 Krishna, what then drives a man to do evil,
against his own will, as if compelled by force?

Shri Krishna replied:
37 It is desire and anger, born of rajas,
which, greedy and wicked, are the enemies here.
38 As smoke conceals fire; caul, the embryo;
and dust a mirror; so these obscure all.
39 Know this unrelenting enemy of the wise, Arjuna,
clouds knowledge in desire's insatiable fire.
40 Senses, mind and intellect are desire's seat;
veiling knowledge through these three,
desire deludes the embodied self.
41 Thus, bull of the Bharatas, first control
the senses, then annihilate this evil
that kills knowledge and discrimination.
42 It is said the five senses are subtle.
But subtler than the senses is the mind;
subtler than the mind is the intellect;
and subtler than intellect is the self.
43 So, knowing what is subtler than intellect,
and restraining self with the self,
strong-armed Prince, kill this enemy,
desire, which is so difficult to destroy.

Thus, in the dialogue between Shri Krishna and Arjuna, on the science of Yoga, part of the knowledge of Brahman, as sung by the Lord in the Upanishad called Bhagavad Gita, ends the third discourse entitled: The Yoga of Action.

Discourse 4

Shri Krishna continued:
1. To Vivasat I taught this immortal yoga.
   Vivasat passed it to Manu, his son;
   and Manu, in turn, to his son Ikshvaku.
2. Thus, Arjuna, imparted in succession,
   this yoga was known by the royal sages,
   but as time passed it withered in this world.
3. This same ancient yoga I have now given you,
   for you are both my devotee and friend,
   and it is truly a matchless mystery.

Arjuna said:
4. But your birth is more recent than Vivasat's.
   How then may I believe, Shri Krishna,
   that in ages past this yoga was taught by you?

Shri Krishna replied:
5. Arjuna, we have both had many births.
   I remember all mine; you know none.
6. Though I am unborn, have an unending self,
   and am Lord of all beings, I am born
   by my yogamaya, through modulating my prakriti.
7. Whenever right wanes and wrong prevails,
   Arjuna, know that I am born again.
8. From age to age, I am reborn in this world,
   to protect the good, destroy the wicked,
   and re-establish the path of dharma.
9. Arjuna, my birth and actions are a mystery.
   Who divines their secret is not reborn

on leaving the body, but comes instead to me.
10 Released from fear, passion and anger,
absorbed in and wholly depending on me,
purified by the penance of knowledge,
many seekers have become one with me.
11 However men approach me, so I accept them;
for all tread my path, whatever way they walk.
12 Men worship the gods to obtain action's fruit;
know such fruit is quickly acquired in this world.
13 The four castes were created by me
through the gunas and karmic interaction.
Yet, while I did this, I do not do.
14 No actions stain me, for I crave no fruit;
nor do actions bind those who understand me.
15 Ancient seekers acted in knowledge of this;
act now as they did, in days long ago.
16 What then is action? What non-action?
Even the wise get confused over this.
Thus I shall teach the truth of action
that you may be freed of its evil effects.
17 Action, illicit action and non-action:
each must be known, for action's ways are complex.
18 Who perceives non-action in action,
action in non-action, is wise among men.
A yogi he is, who knows how to work.
19 He whose work is not driven by desire,
who burns his actions in knowledge's fire—
even the wise pronounce him a sage.
20 Who renounces attachment to action's fruit,
who depends on nothing and is ever content,
though always in action, he does not act.
21 Desiring nothing, mind and body subdued,
surrendering all sense of possession,
he acts in the body and incurs no sin.
22 Satisfied with what may chance to fall,
transcending the opposites, jealous of none,

	unwavering in success and failure,

      whenever he acts, he is not bound.

23 He is free, karma dissolved, who is non-attached,
whose mind in knowledge is soundly based,
and who offers his work as sacrifice.

24 The offering is Brahman; the oblation Brahman;
Brahman is poured into the fire of Brahman—
Brahman, the goal for who sees action as Brahman.

25 Some yogis sacrifice to worship the gods;
others sacrifice their sacrifice itself,
pouring it into the fire which is Brahman.

26 Some sacrifice the sense of hearing,
and all other senses, in the fires of restraint;
others sacrifice sound itself, and all other
sense objects, in the fires of the senses.

27 Others sacrifice all sense activity,
and also their vital energy, in yoga's fire
of self-restraint, ignited by knowledge.

28 Some sacrifice material possessions,
some offer austerity, some yogic practice,
and some learn and teach knowledge acquired
from sacred texts—all these keep austere vows.

29 Some sacrifice outward in inward breath;
some sacrifice inward in outward breath;
some restrain both inward and outward breath flow;

30 and some, their diets under strict control,
sacrifice one vital breath in another.
Each of these well knows what sacrifice is;
by such sacrifices their impurities are purged.

31 Arjuna, whoever eats that which remains
after sacrifice attains to Brahman.
This world is not for the non-sacrificer;
how then, for him, may any other world be?

32 The Vedas describe many forms of sacrifice;
all involve the actions of mind, body and senses.
Know the truth of this and be released.

33   Prefer knowledge sacrifice to that of material things,
for all action has knowledge at its core.

34   To understand this, approach one who knows.
Bow to him, serve him, question him closely;
that wise seer will impart this knowledge.

35   Arjuna, when this knowledge has been attained,
you will never again suffer delusion;
you will see all beings in yourself, then in me.

36   Though you were the most corrupt of sinners,
this knowledge is a boat to traverse all your sins.

37   For as a fierce fire reduces branches to ash,
so fiery knowledge transforms all action to ash.

38   Nothing in this world purifies like knowledge;
who is perfected by yoga will find it within.

39   The dedicated seeker, full of faith,
his senses mastered, acquires knowledge,
and so soon achieves supreme peace.

40   But the doubt-filled, lacking faith, are lost.
For he who doubts, there cannot be this world,
nor that beyond, and never happiness.

41   No action binds he whose self is mastered,
who uses yoga to detach from action,
and whose doubt is razed by knowledge.

42   Therefore, Arjuna, this doubt, born
of ignorance that eats away at your heart,
sever with the sword of self-knowledge.
Adopting this yoga, Bharata—stand!

Thus, in the dialogue between Shri Krishna and Arjuna, on the science of Yoga, part of the knowledge of Brahman, as sung by the Lord in the Upanishad called Bhagavad Gita, ends the fourth discourse entitled: The Yoga of Knowledge, Action and Renunciation.

Discourse 5

Arjuna said:
1. Krishna, you laud renunciation of action;
yet you praise, too, action's performance.
Tell me for certain which is preferred.

Shri Krishna replied:
2. Understand the supreme goal is attained
both by action's renunciation and performance.
But karmayoga is preferred to sanyasa.
3. That one who retains no likes nor dislikes
is truly renounced; free of the opposites,
Arjuna, he easily finds release.
4. The foolish, not the wise, see different ends
to sankhya and yoga; whoever in one
is firmly established receives fruit of both.
5. The sankhya's state is the yogi's goal too;
he who sees both paths as one, truly sees.
6. Yet without yoga, sanyasa is difficult
to achieve; whereas by practising
this yoga, Brahman is quickly attained.
7. That yogi who has conquered his mind,
whose senses are mastered, who is pure within,
who through atman is one with all the world,
although he acts, remains untainted.
8. While the sankhya who perceives reality—
though seeing, hearing, touching or smelling;
though eating, walking, sleeping or breathing;
9. though talking, releasing, grasping or blinking—

he knows that really he does nothing;
the senses only move among their objects.

10 He who practises non-attachment,
offering his actions to Brahman, is not tainted
by sin, just as the lotus leaf sheds water.

11 The yogi uses body, senses, mind and intellect
in actions performed without attachment,
for the purpose of purifying the self.

12 By offering the fruits of all his actions,
the yogi obtains everlasting peace.
But he whose actions are full of desire,
attached to action's rewards, remains bound.

13 The self-controlled sankhya, neither doing
nor causing others to do for him,
mindfully regulates his body's nine gates
within which he contentedly dwells.

14 The Lord neither initiates nor manages
humanity's actions, nor relates action
to its fruit; prakriti alone acts.

15 The Lord accepts no one's virtues or failings;
but ignorance conceals this knowledge,
leaving all humanity deluded.

16 Yet he whose ignorance is dispelled by knowledge
finds that, sun-like, knowledge reveals the Supreme.

17 He whose intellect and mind are passive to that,
and whose self is wholly immersed in that,
finds his sins erased by knowledge and reaches
that state in which there is no rebirth.

18 The wise regard a humble, learned Brahman,
a cow, an elephant, a dog and a dog-eater
with an equal and unbiased eye.

19 He whose mind embraces impartiality,
in this earthly existence conquers creation.
Just as Brahman is perfect and impartial,
so are those who are established in Brahman.

20 He who knows Brahman, and in Brahman rests,

| | his intellect secure, free of delusion,
is neither pleased with the pleasant
nor disturbed by the unpleasant. |
| --- | --- |
| 21 | He whose self is detached from sense objects
knows inner joy; his self one with Brahman
through yoga's practice, he finds eternal bliss within. |
| 22 | But joys born of sense contacts are the source
of misery; since they begin and end,
Arjuna, the wise do not delight in them. |
| 23 | Who in this life, before the body is cast off,
detaches from the floods of desire and anger,
is a yogi; he knows happiness. |
| 24 | He is a yogi who finds happiness
and delight within, who is lit by light within;
one with Brahman, he enters Brahman-nirvana. |
| 25 | Seers whose sins are erased enter the bliss
of Brahman-nirvana; their minds mastered,
doubts dissolved, they gladly serve all beings. |
| 26 | Those ascetics, free of desire and anger,
thoughts controlled, experiencing atman,
find Brahman-nirvana all around them. |
| 27 | He who shuts out all external sense-contacts,
sits with his gaze fixed between his brows,
the nostrils' in and outward breath steadied, |
| 28 | senses, mind and intellect held in control,
intent on freedom, without desire, fear or anger,
is a sagacious seeker who will find liberation. |
| 29 | Whoever knows me, the acceptor of sacrifice
and austerity, the Lord of all the worlds,
the friend of all beings—that one finds peace. |

Thus, in the dialogue between Shri Krishna and Arjuna, on the science of Yoga, part of the knowledge of Brahman, as sung by the Lord in the Upanishad called Bhagavad Gita, ends the fifth discourse entitled: The Yoga of Sacrifice.

Discourse 6

The Lord said:

1. He who does his duty, not seeking its fruit,
is both a sanyasi and yogi; but not he who
neglects the sacrificial fire, nor declines to act.
2. Arjuna, what is called sanyasa
is also yoga, for none becomes a yogi
who does not renounce worldly concerns.
3. For he who wishes to scale yoga's heights,
action is said to be a stepping stone;
when at last he is established in yoga,
tranquil repose is held to be the way.
4. When a man ceases to be attached
to sense objects, or to any action,
being rid of worldly and selfish motives,
he is said to have scaled yoga's heights.
5. Your self, by your self, must lift your self up,
and not allow your self to fall; for only your self
is your friend, only your self is your enemy.
6. One's self is a friend when self conquers the self;
but the self, not conquered by the self, is an enemy.
7. The supreme self of the self-mastered man
remains serene and composed through hot and cold,
joy and sorrow, honour and infamy.
8. That yogi whose self embraces knowledge
and discrimination, who is ever unmoved,
whose senses are mastered, and who recognizes
the real value of earth, stone and gold,
may truthfully be called realised.
9. He stands supreme who regards equally

	friends, foes, supporters, strangers, arbitrators, relatives, foreigners, saints and sinners.
10	The disciplined yogi, living in seclusion, alone, devoid of desires and possessions, should focus attention on his self within.
11	In a clean place, on a seat neither high nor low, that seat covered with kusha grass, on it a deerskin then a cloth placed,
12	sitting with his mind concentrated, thoughts and sense perceptions controlled, he should practise yoga for self-purification.
13	Holding body, head and neck straight and steady, his gaze fixed on the tip of the nose, unmoving, not diverting his eyes,
14	tranquil, fearless, mind restrained, adhering to the brahmacharya's vow, the yogi should sit, thought fixed, wholly absorbed in me.
15	The yogi who thus disciplines his self attains the supreme nirvana which is me.
16	Arjuna, this yoga is not for he who overeats, nor excessively fasts, nor who sleeps too much, nor is always awake.
17	This yoga, by which one transcends all troubles, is only accomplished by he who is contained in diet and recreation, whose waking, sleeping and actions are balanced.
18	When the disciplined mind rests in atman alone, and desire for objects no longer exists, it is said that one is settled in yoga.
19	As a light does not flicker in a windless place, so the mind is likened to be of that yogi who practises unity with atman.
20	When his thought, stilled by yoga, wholly ceases, and the self exults in atman perceiving Atman;
21	when, beyond the senses, his purified intellect apprehends endless bliss

     and, fixed in this state, does not move from it;
22 when, experiencing this, he considers
there exists no greater to be experienced,
and he knows that established in it,
no sorrow could unseat him from it—
23 this state is called yoga, which severs
all union with sorrow; know it should be
practised serenely, but with staunch intent.
24 Renouncing desires born of worldly thinking,
restraining his senses which would grab all around,
25 mind controlled by the power of his will,
by degrees, he resolutely quietens within.
Mind fixed on atman, he does not think at all.
26 When the impulsive mind chases
random objects of thought, it should
be pulled back and refocused on atman.
27 Supreme bliss arrives for that stainless yogi
whose mind is tranquil and passions subdued,
for he becomes one with Brahman.
28 The purified yogi, merged with Atman,
feels the endless bliss of bonding with Brahman.
29 He who practises yoga sees all equally,
perceiving Atman in all beings,
and all beings existing in Atman.
30 He who sees me present in all beings,
and all beings present in me, is not
absent from me, nor am I absent from him.
31 That yogi who, settled in unity,
worships me residing in all beings,
however he acts, he acts in me.
32 Arjuna, he who, measuring himself
against other beings, sees all as one,
viewing each being's joy and sorrow equally,
is considered to be the supreme yogi.

Arjuna said:

33 Krishna, I cannot see this yoga of equality
that you have so clearly described,
as lasting, due to instability.

34 For the mind is restless, turbulent, stubborn,
and overpowering; it is, Krishna,
as difficult to control as the wind.

The Lord replied:

35 Arjuna, no doubt the mind is restless
and hard to rein in; yet by constant practice,
and by vairagya, it can be controlled.

36 Yes, this yoga is difficult to achieve
for he whose self is not controlled;
but he will achieve it, I am sure,
who strives in practice and controls his self.

Arjuna said:

37 Tell me, Krishna, what becomes of him who,
though faithful, has not developed self-control,
and because his mind diverts from practice,
fails to achieve perfection in yoga?

38 Strayed from the path that leads to Brahman,
fallen from both yoga and heaven-seeking ritual,
is he not lost, like evaporating cloud?

39 Please address my misgivings, Krishna, for
only you have the power to destroy my doubts.

Shri Krishna answered:

40 There is no downfall for him, here or beyond;
no one who does good ever meets an evil end.

41 Arjuna, one who has fallen from yoga
enters the heaven reserved for righteous men,
and after dwelling there for many years,
is born to a house of piety and wealth.

42 He may even be born to a family of yogis,

though such a birth is rare in this world.
43 Then, Arjuna, he recovers that insight
which in previous births he achieved,
and struggles towards perfection again.
44 In spite of himself, he is driven
by practice done in former lives, and so
again is drawn to yoga, to seek Brahman
which transcends the Vedas' prescriptions.
45 Hence, that yogi, if he consistently strives,
is perfected through the efforts of many births;
cleansed of stains, he attains the supreme state.
46 The yogi is superior to the ascetic,
greater than sages of book-based knowledge,
and superior to those caught up in action.
Therefore, Arjuna, become a yogi!
47 But of all yogis, he who faithfully worships me,
and whose self is absorbed in me,
I declare to be the supreme yogi.

Thus, in the dialogue between Shri Krishna and Arjuna, on the science of Yoga, part of the knowledge of Brahman, as sung by the Lord in the Upanishad called Bhagavad Gita, ends the sixth discourse entitled: The Yoga of Steadfast, Concentrated Meditation on Atman.

Discourse 7

The Lord said:
1. Now hear, Arjuna, how, by practising yoga,
with mind focused on the sole refuge, me,
you will know me completely and beyond all doubt.
2. I shall impart to you knowledge of both
the manifest and the unmanifest; learn of these
and in all the world nothing remains to be known.
3. Scarcely one in thousands seeks realization;
of those, perhaps one knows my reality.
4. Earth, water, fire, air, ether, mind, intellect,
ego—eightfold is my prakriti divided.
5. But this is my lower aspect, Arjuna;
learn too of my higher aspect, jiva,
by which the whole world is sustained.
6. Know all existence from these two springs;
I am both source and end of all.
7. Nothing is greater than me, Arjuna;
this world is as beads, threaded on me.
8. I am the thirst-quench in water, the light in sun
and moon, and the sacred syllable Om in the Vedas;
the sound in ether, the masculinity in men am I.
9. In earth, I am the sweet fragrance;
in fire, the radiance; in beings, the life-force;
in ascetics, the austerity am I.
10. Know me as the imperishable seed of all beings,
as the acumen within intelligence,
and as the magnificence of the magnificent.
11. Know that in the strong I am the strength
which is free of desire and infatuation;

in all beings, I am lawful sexual desire.

12 Know whatever is born of sattva, rajas
and tamas, manifests from me alone.
Yet, I do not exist in them; they exist in me.

13 Deluded by the gunas' manifestations,
the world fails to recognise me,
the imperishable One who transcends these three.

14 For my baffling maya, woven from
the gunas, is difficult to pierce;
only they tear the veil who take refuge in me.

15 But those who do not take refuge in me,
their knowledge swept away by maya,
deluded, evil, the basest of men,
embrace a demonic way of living.

16 Four wise types, Arjuna, turn towards me:
seekers of wealth, seekers of knowledge,
those shocked by the impact of suffering,
and that one established in knowledge.

17 Of these, the knowing one excels.
Because he is singly devoted to me,
I am dear to him—and he is dear to me.

18 All four are noble, but the knowing one
I view as my self; self-disciplined,
only he is fixed on me, the supreme goal.

19 After experiencing many births,
he at last realizes that Vasudeva is all.
Yet very rare is that exceptional one.

20 The rest, drained of knowledge by diverse
desires, driven by their own natures,
devote themselves to other gods, performing
those rituals and rules designed for each.

21 Yet whatever form the faithful devotee
chooses to worship, know I ensure
that devotee's faith becomes firmly fixed.

22 Filled with faith, worshipping his chosen form,
my power makes certain that, through this form,

	the worshipper receives what he desires.
23	But the fruit these shallow ones gain is short-lived, for those who worship the gods go to the gods; while those who worship me, come to me.
24	The ignorant, not knowing my transcendent, imperishable and supreme Being, think I possess a definite form.
25	Veiled by my yogamaya, I am not perceived by all; thus me, unborn and unchanging, the baffled world fails to see.
26	Arjuna, I know all beings, past, present, and to come; but none truly knows me.
27	All creatures at birth, bewildered by identification, become deluded by the opposites born of likes and dislikes.
28	But the virtuous, who no longer sin, and who are not deluded by the opposites, adopt a life of unwavering devotion to me.
29	Those who focus their existence on me, and strive for freedom from old age and death, come to understand the reality of Brahman, adhyatma and karma.
30	Their wisdom ensures they know me, too, as adhibhuta, adhidaiva and Adhiyajna. Possessed of stable minds, at the stroke of death, their knowledge of me remains firm.

Thus, in the dialogue between Shri Krishna and Arjuna, on the science of Yoga, part of the knowledge of Brahman, as sung by the Lord in the Upanishad called Bhagavad Gita, ends the seventh discourse entitled: The Yoga of Knowledge of the Manifest and Unmanifest.

Discourse 8

Arjuna asked:
1 Krishna, what is Brahman? What adhyatma?
What karma, adhibhuta and adhidaiva?
2 Who is Adhiyajna, and how, in this body,
does he dwell? And by what means, at the stroke
of death, do the stable-minded know you?

The Lord replied:
3 The supreme imperishable is Brahman,
adhyatma, its individual selves;
karma, the process by which they emanate;
4 adhibhuta is all manifest perishable forms;
adhidaiva, the purusha in those forms;
and Adhiyajna, best of the embodied,
dwelling in the body, purified by sacrifice, is me.
5 He, who at the moment death strikes,
departs the body focused on me alone,
attains to me; of this, there is no doubt.
6 That in which a man's mind is ever-absorbed,
he remembers, too, the moment death strikes;
so to that, Arjuna, he surely goes.
7 Therefore, think at all times of me, yet fight;
for, mind and intellect focused on me,
you assuredly will come to me.
8 Arjuna, he whose mind is disciplined
by yoga's practice, whose thoughts never wander,
who in meditation constantly engages,
attains the supreme, divine Purusha.
9 He who meditates on the percipient

        ageless Ruler, the inconceivable Sustainer,
that resplendent Sun beyond all darkness
which is subtler than the subtlest,

10   at the moment death strikes, his mind undisturbed,
by yoga fixing the life-breath between both brows,
will assuredly go to the supreme Purusha.

11   What those who know the Vedas call imperishable,
the reality non-attached ascetics enter,
desiring which they practise brahmachary—
that goal I shall briefly explain to you.

12   That one, who having closed all gates, mind locked
in the heart, life-breath fixed in the head,
remaining stable in yogic meditation,

13   concentrated on me, then departs the body
uttering Om, Brahman's sacred syllable,
will surely achieve the supreme goal.

14   Arjuna, he, who maintains a one-pointed mind
which is ever focused and absorbed in me,
is a yogi by whom I am easily attained.

15   Great beings, achieving the highest perfection,
and having come to me, are not reborn
into this transient world of sorrow.

16   All worlds are subject, from Brahmaloka down,
to decay and return; but, Arjuna,
there is no rebirth for those who come to me.

17   Those yogis who know Brahma's day lasts
a thousand yuga, and his night a thousand
yuga more, understand the true nature of time.

18   All beings manifest from the unmanifest
at the birth of cosmic day; at cosmic night,
they merge with the unmanifest again.

19   Arjuna, this same multitude of beings
is repeatedly, and by their very nature, reborn,
dissolving at the dusk of cosmic night,
and reborn with the dawn of cosmic day.

20   Yet much higher than this unmanifest

      exists another endless Unmanifest,
which, when all perishes, is not destroyed.

21 That Unmanifest, called imperishable,
is known as the ultimate goal; those who
reach it never return to this world,
for it is my supreme abode.

22 Arjuna, that supreme unmanifest Purusha,
which pervades all, in which all beings dwell,
is attained through undivided devotion.

23 The conditions controlling a yogi's return,
and those controlling his non-return,
I shall now describe to you, bull of the Bharatas.

24 Fire, light, the bright fortnight, the sun's six-month
northern course—who by these departing,
who also know Brahman, attain to Brahman.

25 Smoke, night, the dark fortnight, the sun's six-month
southern course—that yogi by these departing,
whose actions were performed with attachment,
attains the lunar light, and then returns.

26 Bright and dark—these two are deemed the eternal
paths of the world; by the one a man returns,
but by the other he has no return.

27 Arjuna, the yogi able to discriminate
between these two paths is never deluded.
Therefore, at all times be steadfast in yoga.

28 The yogi who understands all this
transcends the fruit accrued from austerity,
sacrifice, charity and studying the Vedas,
and attains the primal supreme state.

Thus, in the dialogue between Shri Krishna and Arjuna, on the science of Yoga, part of the knowledge of Brahman, as sung by the Lord in the Upanishad called Bhagavad Gita, ends the eighth discourse entitled: The Yoga of Brahman.

Discourse 9

The Lord said:

1. To you who lacks malice, I shall further unfold
the secret knowledge of the manifest and unmanifest,
knowing which you will be freed from all sorrow.

2. This knowledge is king of all sciences,
king of all secrets; easy to practise,
it is the premium purifier, the essence of dharma;
learned by direct experience, it is immutable.

3. Arjuna, those who lack faith in this teaching
do not reach me, but retread this path of death.

4. The world is pervaded by my unmanifest Being;
all beings are in me, I am not in them.

5. And yet, all beings are not in me.
Behold my divine power; though creator
and sustainer of all, my self dwells in none.

6. As strong winds, blowing everywhere,
are yet contained in the subtle ether,
know all beings are contained within me.

7. When a kalpa ends, all beings merge with my prakriti;
when the next begins, I project them out again.

8. Using my prakriti, again and again
I manifest this multitude of beings,
each subject to its own prakriti.

9. Yet these actions, Arjuna, do not bind me,
standing separate and non-attached.

10. With me as presiding witness, prakriti manifests
all beings, whether moving or unmoving—
thus the wheel of the world is kept turning.

11. Not knowing my transcendent being

is born within the human form, fools spurn me,
the sovereign Lord of all beings.

12 Their knowledge and actions filled with futile hopes,
these unthinking and deluded creatures
possess a monstrous, bedevilled nature.

13 But great beings, embracing the divine nature,
know me as the imperishable source of all;
they worship me with a one-pointed mind.

14 Ever striving, with unwavering faith,
these devotees bow repeatedly to me,
their worship wholly focused on me.

15 Others, in knowledge sacrifice, seeing me
everywhere, worship me as one in all beings;
yet others worship me as One beyond all diversity.

16 The Vedic ritual, the sacrifice am I;
the ancestral offering, the herbs am I;
the sacred texts, the ghee, the fire am I;
the offering to the fire am I.

17 I am the sustainer of the world;
I am its father, mother and grandfather.
I am the purifier, the one to be known;
sacred Om, the Rig, Saman and Yujas am I.

18 I am the goal, supporter, lord and witness,
the abode, refuge, friend, origin and end,
storehouse, resting place and imperishable seed.

19 Arjuna, I heat, I pour and withhold rain,
I am eternity and death, existence and extinction.

20 Those who follow the three Vedas, drink juice
of soma to purge themselves of sin, and offer
sacrifices in worship, seek the abode of heaven;
in reward, they reach the realm of the gods,
in heaven tasting the gods' divine joys.

21 That vast realm enjoyed, and all merit spent,
they then return to the world of mortals;
thus those who are devoted to Vedic ritual,
addicted to action's fruit, merely come and go.

22 But those who are devoted to none but me,
   who worship and think only of me,
   I provide with whatever they need.
23 Arjuna, know those who worship
   other gods still worship me alone,
   even if their perspectives are mistaken;
24 for I am the acceptor and Lord of sacrifice,
   but not knowing my reality, they slip.
25 Who worship the gods go to the gods,
   who worship the ancestors go the ancestors,
   who worship ghosts go to the ghosts,
   but who worship me come to me alone.
26 What, with love, a devotee offers me,
   whether leaf, flower, water or fruit,
   that sincere worship I gladly accept.
27 Arjuna, whatever you do or eat,
   whatever you offer as sacrifice,
   austerity or gift, dedicate to me.
28 Practising the yoga of renunciation,
   you shall be released from karma's binding
   good and bad fruit. Freed, you will come to me.
29 Know that I view all beings equally;
   none are hateful to me, to none am I attached.
   Yet of those who devotedly worship me,
   know they abide in me, and I abide in them.
30 If even the greatest sinner worships me
   with one-pointed devotion, he should
   be called a saint, for he has correct intent.
31 Through his virtues, he achieves lasting peace;
   know, Arjuna, that my devotee never falls.
32 Even women, Vaishyas and Sudras,
   and those born into unspiritual homes,
   taking refuge in me, gain the supreme goal.
33 How much more, then, those royal sages
   and pure Brahmans who are devoted to me?
   Thus, since you have entered this transient,

       pain-filled world, ensure you always worship me.
34   Fix your mind on me; be devoted to me;
       offer all your sacrifices and worship to me.
       Do this, attaching yourself to me, holding
       me as your goal, and you shall come to me.

Thus, in the dialogue between Shri Krishna and Arjuna, on the science of Yoga, part of the knowledge of Brahman, as sung by the Lord in the Upanishad called Bhagavad Gita, ends the ninth discourse entitled: The Yoga of the King of Sciences and the King of Secrets.

Discourse 10

The Lord said:

1. Once more, hear my supreme word, Arjuna,
which you, my devotee, I shall tell for your good.
2. Neither gods nor great sages know my origin,
for I am the sole source of them all.
3. Whoever knows me, the supreme Lord
of the world, as birthless and beginningless,
has no delusions and is released from all sin.
4. Intellect, knowledge, freedom from delusion,
fortitude, truthfulness, self-control, serenity,
pleasure, pain, birth, death, fear, fearlessness,
5. non-violence, equanimity, contentment,
austerity, generosity, honour and dishonour—
all these attributes come only from me.
6. The seven great sages, the ancient four,
and the Manus, were born of my mind;
all the world's beings descended from them.
7. Who understands my power and its emanations
becomes steadfastly established in yoga;
of this, there can be no doubt.
8. I am the source of all; all manifests from me.
Knowing this, fully devoted, the wise worship me.
9. Minds fixed on me, organs immersed in me,
teaching each other, my name always on their lips,
each day they are filled with peace and delight.
10. On those who are ever focused on me,
who lovingly worship me, I bestow the yoga
of intellect, by which they may come to me.

11   In compassion, and dwelling in their hearts,
I blast their ignorance with knowledge's light.

Arjuna responded:
12   You are transcendent Brahman, the supreme abode,
the great purifier, the deathless divine being,
the original god, unborn and all-pervading.
13   All the seers declared this: the divine sage
Narada, and Asita, Devala and Vyasa too.
And this truth you have proclaimed to me!
14   Keshava, all you tell me I accept as true;
neither gods nor demons know your manifestations.
15   Creator and ruler of all the world's beings,
God of gods, cosmic Lord, supreme Being,
you alone, by yourself, know your self.
16   Only you can describe your manifestations
and how your power pervades all the worlds.
17   Master of yoga, ever meditating on you,
how may I know you? How am I to think of you?
18   Krishna, in full detail please describe once more
your power and its manifestations,
for I am not sated of your nectar-like words.

The Lord said:
19   Best of the Kurus, I will describe only
the paramount of my manifestations,
for my plenitude possesses no limit.
20   I am Atman, Arjuna, seated in the heart
of every being; of all that exists,
I alone am beginning, middle and end.
21   Of Adityas, I am Vishnu;
of radiant stars, the resplendent sun;
of Maruts, know me to be Marichi;
of night's luminaries, the moon am I.
22   Of the Vedas, I am Sama; of gods, Indra;
of organs, mind; in beings, consciousness am I.

23 Of the destructive Rudras, I am Shankara;
of Yakshas and Rakshasas, Kubera;
of Vasus, fire; of mountains, Meru am I.

24 Of priests, know me to be Brihaspati;
of maharatha, see me as Skanda;
of waters, know that the ocean am I.

25 Of great seers, I am Bhrigu;
of words, the sacred syllable Om;
of sacrifices, know me to be japa;
of immovables, the Himalayas am I.

26 Of trees, I am the sacred Ashvattha;
of divine seers, know me as Narada;
of Gandharvas, I am Chitrarathra;
of perfected ones, austere Kapila am I.

27 Of elephants, I am Airavata;
of horses, the nectar-born Ucchaihshravas;
of men, the sovereign am I.

28 Of weapons, I am the thunderbolt, Vajra;
of cows, know me to be Kamadhenu;
of procreators, I am Kandarpa;
of serpents, eternal Vasuki am I.

29 Of cobras, I am the serpent god, Ananda;
of water born, know me to be Varuna;
of ancestral guardian spirits, I am Aryaman;
of rulers, Yama, the ruler of the dead, am I.

30 Of demons, Prahlada; of measurers, time;
of beasts, the lion; of birds, Garuda am I.

31 Of purifiers, know me as the cleansing wind;
of warriors, the peerless Rama;
of water beasts, I am the crocodile;
of rivers, the sacred Ganges am I.

32 I am beginning, middle and end of all that is.
Arjuna, I am the reason in debate;
of all knowledge, knowledge of the self am I.

33 Of sounds, I am A; of compound words,
know me as the balancing conjunction.

	I am both time that never ends
	and the creator who looks out everywhere.
34	I am death, which devours all; yet also
	the source of all to be. Of feminine virtues,
	fame, wealth, speech, memory, thoughtfulness,
	constancy and forgiveness am I.
35	Of Saman hymns, I am Brihat Saman;
	of metres, Gaytri; of the twelve months,
	Margashirsha; of seasons, Spring am I.
36	Of deceivers, I am the chance in dice.
	The glory in the glorious, the resolve
	in victory, the goodness in the good am I.
37	Of Vrishnis, Vasudeva; of Pandus, Arjuna;
	of sages, Vyasa; of poets, Ushanas am I.
38	The rod of rulers, the tactics of the victorious,
	silence in secrets, what the knowing know am I.
39	Understand, Arjuna, I am the seed
	of all beings; for nothing that is, whether
	moving or still, exists apart from me.
40	My marvellous manifestations have no end;
	know I have but briefly described their range.
41	Whatever emanates good, beauty or power,
	know that is just a fragment of my splendour.
42	Yet, what do you learn from such great detail?
	Know that with but a part of myself, Arjuna,
	I support this whole cosmos as I stand!

Thus, in the dialogue between Shri Krishna and Arjuna, on the science of Yoga, part of the knowledge of Brahman, as sung by the Lord in the Upanishad called Bhagavad Gita, ends the tenth discourse entitled: The Yoga of Supernal Qualities.

Discourse 11

Arjuna proclaimed:
1. By your grace you have spoken profound words,
revealing knowledge of the Supreme,
thanks to which my delusion is shattered.
2. For, lotus-eyed Lord, in detail from you
I have learned of the source and end of all,
and, too, of your imperishable glory.
3. But I long to perceive you in that form
you have just described, as Ishvara.
4. If, master of yoga, you think me able to see it,
reveal to me your glorious supreme form!

The Lord responded:
5. Regard, Partha, in hundreds, in thousands,
my manifold, diversely-shaped and coloured forms.
6. Arjuna, behold the Adityas, Vasus, Rudras,
the twin Ashwins and the Maruts,
and vast numbers more, never revealed before.
7. Perceive, Arjuna, as my body now,
the whole cosmos, animate, inanimate
and everything else you desire to see.
8. Yet, with your own eyes, you cannot see me;
therefore, divine sight I bestow on you.
Behold the divine glory of my yoga!

Sanjaya said:
9. Great King! Shri Krishna, master of yoga,
to Arjuna then revealed his supreme form.
10. Many-mouthed and multi-eyed, of manifold

wondrous attributes, hung with innumerable
celestial ornaments, and wielding
countless uplifted weapons of death,
draped in limitless garlands and vibrant cloths,
11 and wafting intoxicating perfumes;
wholly marvellous, it was the Lord's form,
infinite and cosmic, facing everywhere.
12 The brilliance of a thousand suns exploding
in the heavens together would still not equal
the splendour of that all-pervading Soul!
13 Arjuna perceived the entire cosmos,
wholly diverse, yet concentrated
in one form—the body of the God of gods.
14 Elated and awe-struck, hair on his skin bristling,
Arjuna bowed his head low to the Lord,
and with joined palms addressed him thus:

Arjuna said:
15 Lord, within your body all gods and hosts
of unique and wondrous beings I see:
crowds of rishis, Brahma on his lotus throne,
and writhing coils of celestial serpents.
16 I perceive numberless arms, bellies, faces
and eyes in endless forms surrounding me.
You are so great, cosmic Lord, that I see
neither your end, middle nor beginning.
17 Crowned, armed with massive discuses and clubs,
you flame like a blazing, effulgent sun,
so brilliant my sight is dazed, uncomprehending.
18 You are supreme and imperishable,
the goal of knowledge, the ultimate end of all.
You are the guardian of ageless dharma;
you are, I now understand, eternal Being.
19 You have neither beginning, middle nor end.
Your strength is unlimited; your arms countless;

      your eyes the sun and moon; your mouth a fire
      so radiant it scorches the universe.
20   Universal Soul, you fill the four directions
      between heaven and earth; seeing your
      frightening form, the three worlds quake in fear!
21   Multitudes of gods are entering you.
      Some, awe-struck, have joined their palms in worship,
      while hosts of siddhas and maharishis chant
      and hymn you with melodious song.
22   The massed Rudras, Adityas, and Vasus,
      the Sadhyas, twin Ashwins, Maruts and Manes,
      the Gandharvas, Yaksas, Asuras and siddhas,
      all these, amazed, gaze wondering at you.
23   Dread Lord, on witnessing your colossal form—
      your many mouths and eyes, your immense arms,
      feet and thighs, your countless vast, bulging bellies,
      the terrible teeth in each gnashing jaw—
      all the worlds are terror-struck. And so am I!
24   All-pervading Lord, you stretch past the sky,
      so radiant, so rainbow-hued, your mouths so gaping,
      your dazzling eyes so huge, I shudder within,
      and both my peace and self-restraint flee.
25   I stagger from your frightfully gnashing teeth,
      my chilled heart rigid in my chest, reeling,
      as your mouths breathe flames like the fires of death.
      Be merciful, Lord of the gods, refuge of all!
26   Dhritarastra's sons and serried ranks of kings
      I can see each being eaten by you,
      while Bhishma, Drona and Karna, and all those
27   other great warriors of ours, fall headlong
      into the teeth of your terrible jaws;
      some from those teeth dangle, puny heads crushed.
28   As rivers, in foaming torrents, rush into the sea,
      so these mortal heroes feed your flaming mouths.
29   As moths, frantically flapping, plunge into the flame,

so these pour into your mouths to their deaths.
30 And you, with relish, swallow each of them,
tongues lapping on every fiery side.
Lord, you ignite the cosmos with your splendour;
you burn up all that is with your blazing brilliance!
31 Tell me who you are in such a terrible form.
I bow before you; be benevolent.
For, primal Lord, I wish to know your purpose.

The Lord replied:
32 Time I am, enflamed destroyer of the world,
about to devour all these people here.
Even without your sword, your enemies shall die!
33 Stand, therefore, and win repute;
defeat your foes and enjoy your kingdom.
These warriors are already slain by me;
Arjuna, you will become but an instrument.
34 Drona, Bhishma, Jayadratha, Karna
and these heroic warriors else—all of whom
I have already killed—go out and slaughter.
Do not fear. Victory is yours in battle. Fight!

Sanjaya said:
35 After hearing Keshava's exhortation, Arjuna,
still trembling in fear, joined his palms and bowed.
Again bowing, voice faltering, he spoke to Krishna.

Arjuna said:
36 Inner controller of all, it is right
that the cosmos exults and praises you;
demons, terrified, flee in all directions,
while hosts of siddhas devotedly bow to you.
37 And why, Mahatman, should they not bow?
You are far greater even than Brahma.
Eternal and immutable King of the Gods,

    refuge of the cosmos, you are being,
non-being, and that which transcends both.

38   You are the primal god, the most ancient being,
the last resting place of all which exists.
You are knower and known, the supreme abode;
you pervade the cosmos, Lord of infinite forms.

39   You are Vayu, Yama, Agni and Varuna,
and Shashanka, Prajapati and the Ancient, too.
All hail to you; a thousand times, hail!
Again and again, all hail to you!

40   Lord of all, who is before and behind,
all hail to you! Soul of the cosmos,
you possess infinite potency and strength.
Your power pervades all. For you are all!

41   If, not recognizing your greatness, and thinking
you only a friend, I ever in affection,
or even negligence, have called, "Krishna!",

42   "Yadava!", "Comrade!", or whatever else rudely
I might have said in jest, resting or at meals,
while alone or with others, if I said such to you,
who are endless, I hereby ask your forgiveness.

43   You are father of animate and inanimate.
Revered guru of the whole world,
in the three worlds none is equal to you.
How, then, could any other be greater?

44   Therefore, I prostrate my body to you,
craving your grace, adored Lord of all.
As father with son, as lover with beloved,
as friend with friend, so should you bear with me.

45   Joy fills me to have seen what none else has before;
yet my mind is tormented by fear, too.
Reveal again your glorious form.
Be gracious, King of Gods, refuge of all.

46   I wish to see you as you were before,
crowned, with discuses and clubs in each hand.

> Thousand-armed one, who embodies the cosmos,
> in that four-armed form appear again!

The Lord responded:

47 Arjuna, from favour for you, by my yoga power,
I have shown my radiant, primal, infinite, cosmic form,
which none before you has ever perceived.

48 Not by the Vedas, sacrifice or by studying,
nor by gifts, rituals or strict austerities,
can I be seen in this world in such a form—
only by you, best of the Kurus.

49 At seeing this terrifying form of mine,
do not be baffled or disturbed; free of fear,
calm of mind, see me again in the form I was.

Sanjaya said:

50 So Shri Krishna pronounced to Arjuna,
and showed him again his four-armed form.
Then, resuming his gentle form,
the Mahatman soothed him, terrified once more.

Arjuna said:

51 Krishna, seeing again your benign human form,
I am returned to myself, composure regained.

The Lord concluded:

52 The form you have seen is difficult to view;
even the gods crave to perceive it.

53 Not by studying the Vedas, penance or charity,
nor even by sacrifice, can I be seen in this form.

54 Yet by one-pointed devotion, Arjuna, may I
in this form be seen, known, and attained to.

55 Who diligently performs his work for me,
is ever fixed on and devoted to me,
lives free of attachment, has enmity for none,
know that one alone, Arjuna, comes to me.

Thus, in the dialogue between Shri Krishna and Arjuna, on the science of Yoga, part of the knowledge of Brahman, as sung by the Lord in the Upanishad called Bhagavad Gita, ends the eleventh discourse entitled: The Yoga of the Vision of the Cosmic Form.

Discourse 12

Arjuna asked:
1. Of those disciplined devotees who
always worship you, and those devotees
who worship the unchanging Unmanifest,
which are said to best understand yoga?

The Lord replied:
2. I consider the best yogis to be those
whose focused minds always remember me,
who constantly and faithfully worship me.
3. Those who worship the inconceivable,
omnipresent, indefinable, constant,
immovable, imperishable Unmanifest,
4. whose senses are under full control,
serving all devotedly, even-minded
towards all—they indeed come to me.
5. Yet it is difficult for those whose minds
are fixed always on the Unmanifest,
for it is challenging to sustain oneness
with the Unmanifest while in the body.
6. But those who depend on me, whose yoga
is a constant meditation on me,
and who dedicate all their actions to me,
7. they, Arjuna, thoughts never distracted from me,
I shall save from this ocean of death.
8. Fix your mind on me, therefore; establish
your intellect in me. Let there be no doubt.
Do this, and, assuredly, you shall abide in me.
9. But if you cannot fix a steadied mind on me,

	Arjuna, seek to win me by practising yoga.

10   If constant practice is too hard to maintain,
concentrate on service to me; for by such service,
you will certainly achieve perfection.

11   If you are unable to sustain such
service, dedicate all you do to me,
subdue the self, and abandon action's fruit.

12   Knowledge transcends practice; meditation
is better than knowledge; yet better than
meditation is renouncing action's fruit,
for renunciation leads to peace.

13   Who is hostile towards none, is friendly,
compassionate, eschews thoughts of 'I'
or 'mine', is persevering and patient,
and accepts pain and pleasure alike,

14   who is always content, stable in yoga,
is self-restrained, has firm resolve, and
has yielded mind and intellect to me—
that devotee of mine is dear to me.

15   Who neither disturbs the world, nor is disturbed
by it, who is never excited, resentful, fearful,
nor agitated—that one is dear to me.

16   Who expects nothing, is pure, clear thinking,
impartial and free of distractions,
is not the doer in any action—
that devotee of mine is dear to me.

17   Who fosters no likes or dislikes, neither
desires, nor complains at being without,
and has renounced both good and evil—
that devotee of mine is dear to me.

18   Who treats alike both friend and foe,
who accepts honour and infamy,
heat and cold, pain and pleasure,
and is free of clouding attachments;

19   who receives praise and blame equally,
is silent, content with whatever life deals,

has no sense of possessing a home,
and whose mind is steady and stable—
that devotee of mine is dear to me.

20 But those who are faithful, wholly focused on me,
and who practise this decreed nectar of dharma—
those devotees are very dear to me.

Thus, in the dialogue between Shri Krishna and Arjuna, on the science of Yoga, part of the knowledge of Brahman, as sung by the Lord in the Upanishad called Bhagavad Gita, ends the twelfth discourse entitled: The Yoga of Devotion.

Discourse 13

The Lord said:
1. Arjuna, know this body is the field,
and who knows it is the knower of the field;
thus is he defined by those who know.
2. Know I am the knower of the field in all fields,
and that knowledge of the field, and of
the knower of the field, I view as true knowledge.
3. What the field is, of what it consists,
how it is modified, where it comes from,
who knows it, and the extent of his power—
hear all this briefly from me.
4. Ancient seers have expounded this knowledge
in distinct and various forms: in Vedic hymns,
and the Brahma Sutras, well-reasoned and conclusive.
5. The five elements, ego, intellect,
unmanifest prakriti, the ten organs,
the mind, and the senses' five objects,
6. likes and dislikes, pleasure and pain, the body's
inter-linked organs, awareness, cohesion—
this, in short, is the field and its extent.
7. Freedom from hypocrisy and pride,
non-violence, forgiveness, honesty,
obedience to the guru, purity, stability,
8. self-restraint, detachment from sense objects,
absence of egotism, understanding
of the painfulness of birth, death, aging,
9. and disease, non-attachment, no sense
of possession of children, spouse or home,
equanimity in the face of good and ill fortune,

10 persevering, focused devotion to me,
a resorting to secluded places,
avoiding the distractions of the crowd,
11 understanding the nature of atman
and recognizing wisdom's true goal—all this
is called knowledge, and all else is ignorance.
12 I shall now speak of what is to be known:
the supreme, beginningless Brahman, which is
said to possess neither being nor non-being;
knowing it, immortality is gained.
13 Its countless feet walking and hands clasping,
its head, mouth, ears and eyes filling all space,
it penetrates the entire cosmos.
14 Though perceiving sense objects, it has no senses;
though touching nothing, it sustains all;
though attributeless, it experiences the gunas.
15 It is within all beings, yet also outside;
it stands still, but is always moving;
so subtle it can never be conceived,
it is distant, yet always very close.
16 Though undivided, it seems to exist
divided in all beings; known as the Preserver,
it also creates and devours all that is.
17 Light of lights, it is said to exist beyond darkness;
it is knowledge, the goal of knowledge,
known by knowledge, seated in the hearts of all.
18 Thus is briefly expounded the field,
knowledge, and that which is to be known.
When my devotee knows these, he enters into me.
19 Know purusha and prakriti are beginningless;
the gunas and all modulations are born of prakriti.
20 Prakriti is the cause of all organs
and effects; know purusha is the cause
of the experience of pleasure and pain.
21 Purusha, seated in prakriti,
experiences the gunas produced by prakriti;

attachment to the gunas then causes
purusha's birth in good or evil homes.

22 Know atman, seated within this body,
is called the witness, guide, sustainer,
experiencer, great lord and supreme self.

23 Who knows purusha, prakriti and
the gunas' modulations, is assured
of not being born again, however he acts.

24 Some perceive the self in the self, their self
honed by meditation; others achieve
by sankhyayoga or karmayoga.

25 Still others, though not knowing for themselves,
yet comprehend on hearing from those who do;
adhering to what they hear, they too escape death.

26 Arjuna, whatever is born, standing
or moving, know it derives from the union
of field and the knower of the field.

27 Who perceives the supreme Lord
as the one imperishable abiding
in all perishable beings—he truly sees.

28 Who perceives the supreme Lord
as equally present everywhere,
and does not hurt his self through his self—
he achieves the transcendent state.

29 Who perceives that prakriti performs all actions,
and that atman does not act—he truly sees.

30 When one perceives that diverse beings
abide in One, from which all that is emanates,
one attains to the oneness of Brahman.

31 Arjuna, this imperishable, beginningless,
supreme atman, which transcends the gunas,
though in the body, neither acts nor is stained.

32 As pervasive ether is too subtle to be soiled,
so atman, seated in the body, is not sullied.

33 As one sun illuminates the whole world,
so the field's Lord lights the entire field.

34   Therefore, whoever with the eye of knowledge
        discerns between field and knower of the field,
        and knows how beings are released from prakriti—
        he, Arjuna, attains to the Supreme.

Thus, in the dialogue between Shri Krishna and Arjuna, on the science of Yoga, part of the knowledge of Brahman, as sung by the Lord in the Upanishad called Bhagavad Gita, ends the thirteenth discourse entitled: The Yoga of Discriminating Between the Field and the Knower of the Field.

Discourse 14

The Lord said:
1. I shall expound again the highest knowledge,
the supreme wisdom, knowing which all sages
transcend the world and achieve perfection.
2. Who practise this knowledge become one with me;
at cosmic dawn they are not reborn,
and at cosmic dusk they do not dissipate.
3. In my womb of prakriti I place the seed;
from this all beings come to birth.
4. Arjuna, whatever is born, the womb
is prakriti, and I the seed-giving father am.
5. Sattva, rajas and tamas—these gunas,
Bharata, spring from prakriti and bind
imperishable atman to the body.
6. Of these, sattva, stainless by nature,
illuminates and purifies—sinless one,
it binds with the bonds of knowledge and joy.
7. Rajas, by nature energetic,
know as the source of thirst and attachment—
it binds with the bonds of action.
8. And know tamas, born of ignorance,
deludes those who see the body as the self—
it binds with inattention, lethargy and sleep.
9. Sattva attaches man to happiness;
rajas to action; and tamas, Arjuna,
obscuring all knowledge, to distraction.
10. Sattva reigns when rajas and tamas decline;
rajas when sattva and tamas go down;
tamas when sattva and rajas diminish.

11   When the light of knowledge shines from
the body's gates, know sattva has risen.
12   But when rajas ascends, Arjuna, then greed,
bustling activity, impatience, appetites,
and immersion in action appear.
13   And when denseness, laziness, delusion
and neglect of duty rise, know tamas rules.
14   He who meets death when sattva reigns gains
those unstained worlds attained by noble men;
15   if when rajas prevails, he is born among
those attached to action; if when tamas
dominates, he is born among the unknowing.
16   The fruit of sattvika action is stainless merit;
that of rajas, pain; of tamas, ignorance.
17   Knowledge is born of sattva; greed, of rajas;
neglect, delusion and ignorance, of tamas.
18   Those abiding in sattva rise upwards;
those in rajas remain in the middle;
while those in tamas sink into the depths.
19   When the seer knows none but the gunas acts,
and perceives that which stands beyond those three,
he assuredly comes to my supreme state.
20   Transcending the gunas which form the body,
he is released from birth, age, death and pain,
and attains to the deathless state.

Arjuna asked:
21   How is he marked who transcends the gunas?
Tell me, Lord, what is his conduct?
And how does he rise beyond the gunas?

The Lord said:
22   Arjuna, he who, when they are present,
does not flee from light, activity or delusion,
nor yet desires them when they have gone;
23   who, seated like a witness, unwavering, firm,

	unruffled by the gunas, knows they alone act;
24	who is self-controlled, even-minded, and accepts alike pleasure and pain, censure and praise, seeing earth, stone and gold for what they are;
25	who is unchanged in honour and infamy, acts evenly always to friend and foe, and is not the doer whatever the action— he is said to have transcended the gunas.
26	He who, through bhaktiyoga, always worships me, transcends the gunas and is worthy of Brahman.
27	For I am the ground of Brahman itself, the imperishable and immortal foundation of eternal dharma and perfect bliss.

Thus, in the dialogue between Shri Krishna and Arjuna, on the science of Yoga, part of the knowledge of Brahman, as sung by the Lord in the Upanishad called Bhagavad Gita, ends the fourteenth discourse entitled: The Yoga of Identifying the Three Guna's Qualities.

Discourse 15

The Lord said:
1. With its root above, branches here below,
and sacred songs as leaves, they say the Ashvattha
is imperishable; who knows it, knows the Vedas.
2. Fed by the gunas, its shoots sense-objects,
its branches spread above and below; its roots,
entwining actions, tangle the world of men.
3. Yet such a form is not perceivable here,
not its beginning, end nor foundation.
To see, first this firmly rooted Ashvattha
must be felled with the axe of detachment.
4. The supreme state should then be sought,
attaining to which there is no return,
and refuge found in the primal Being
from which this emanated cosmos flows.
5. Free of pride and delusion, desires ceased,
the taints of attachments removed,
harmonized with Atman, released from pain
and pleasure, unmoved by the opposites,
these wise ones attain the highest haven.
6. Neither sun, moon nor fire illuminate it,
and none who reaches it ever returns;
such, Arjuna, is my eternal abode.
7. Eternal jiva, of myself a particle,
in this body draws around itself the senses
and mind, prakriti their foundation.
8. As the wind carries scents from flower-beds,
so the lord of the body takes these six
when it discards one body and travels on.

9   Dwelling in hearing, sight, touch, taste, smell,
and mind, it, through them, savours sense objects.

10   The ignorant can never perceive this
which dwells in and departs from the body,
and which via the gunas enjoys sense objects.
Only those with the eye of knowledge perceive it.

11   Striving yogis perceive it in their self;
the ignorant, inwardly impure,
do not see it, however hard they strive.

12   Know that light which blazes from the sun
to illuminate the world, which radiates too
from fire and the moon, is wholly mine.

13   Entering soil, my strength sustains all beings;
as the nectar-like moon, I feed all plants.

14   Becoming the vaishvanara fire,
I lodge in all bodies; united with breath,
I consume the four varieties of food.

15   I am seated in the hearts of all; from me
come memory, knowledge and doubt's death.
It is I in the Vedas who is to be known;
yet am I the author of Vedanta,
and he who knows the Vedas too.

16   There are two types of being in the world:
perishable and imperishable.
Know all creatures are perishable,
and imperishable that from which they derive.

17   Yet the supreme being is other than these.
Called Paramatman, as deathless Ishvara
it pervades and sustains all three worlds.

18   Because I transcend both the perishable
and the imperishable, I am known
as Purushotthama in the Vedas and world.

19   The wise who know me as Purushotthama
know all there is to know, Arjuna;
they worship me with their whole being.

20   Know, sinless one, I have revealed to you

this most secret teaching, knowing which
you become wise, your life's purpose fulfilled.

Thus, in the dialogue between Shri Krishna and Arjuna, on the science of Yoga, part of the knowledge of Brahman, as sung by the Lord in the Upanishad called Bhagavad Gita, ends the fifteenth discourse entitled: The Yoga of Purushotthama.

Discourse 16

The Lord said:
1. Lack of fear, inner purity, charity,
consistency in practice and knowledge of yoga,
self-restraint, sacrificial service,
study of Vedic texts, austerity, honesty,
2. non-violence, truthfulness, composure,
absence of anger, cavilling and greed,
compassion, kindness, modesty, stability,
3. vigour, forgiveness, determination,
uprightness, absence of enmity or pride—
Bharata, these characteristics exist
in one who is born with divine qualities.
4. Hypocrisy, arrogance, self-importance,
anger, incivility, ignorance—these exist
in one born with demonic qualities.
5. Divine qualities lead to liberation,
the demonic to bondage. Do not fear, Arjuna,
for you were born with a divine heritage.
6. Only two types of beings inhabit
this world: the divine and the demonic.
Arjuna, as the divine has been well-described,
now hear of the demonic in detail from me.
7. The demonic lack knowledge of correct
and incorrect action, possessing neither
integrity, morality nor truthfulness.
8. "The world has no truth, moral base or Lord,"
such proclaim, "and birth results only from lust."
9. Set in this stance, their thinking blinkered,
having lost themselves, they execute terrible acts,

becoming the world's enemies, destroying it.
10 Driven by insatiable desires,
filled with hypocrisy, conceit and arrogance,
ignorantly embracing deluded ideas,
these men of vile doctrines stamp through the world.
11 Given to the countless cares which end only
at death, devoted to sensual pleasure
which they believe is everything, bound by
12 the countless traps of vanity and hope,
giving themselves up to anger and lust,
they unjustly hoard wealth to feed their desires.
13 "Look how much I have grabbed today;
yet I have more ambitions. This is my wealth;
but there is so much more out there to be added.
14 I destroyed that enemy; I shall many more.
I am a lord; I enjoy it; I deserve all
of my power, success and happiness.
15 I am wealthy, born to a noble family.
Who compares to me? I will make sacrifice!
I will give alms! And I shall enjoy myself!"
16 Blinded by their ignorance, flung between
numerous fantasies, twisting in delusion's web,
addicted to their appetites, they fall into a fetid hell.
17 Self-conceited and wilful, intoxicated
by status and wealth, they hypocritically offer
sacrifices for show, ignoring the rituals' intent.
18 Driven by pride, violence, arrogance, lust and anger,
they even scorn me in their own and others' bodies.
19 These cruel, sinful sneerers, vile among men,
I repeatedly hurl back into the world,
Arjuna, to be born into demonic homes.
20 Deluded, they are far from reaching me.
Instead, entering a demonic existence,
birth after birth, they sink ever more lowly.
21 Desire, anger and greed—these triple gates of hell
usher them to ruin. Shun all three, therefore.

22 Only those who avoid these gates of hell
have the chance to do what is right for the self,
and thereafter achieve the supreme state.
23 But he who ignores the scriptures, and follows
the course dictated by his desires, attains neither
perfection, happiness nor the supreme goal.
24 Therefore, let the sacred texts be your authority
to determine what to do or not do.
Study them, and act according to their guidance.

Thus, in the dialogue between Shri Krishna and Arjuna, on the science of Yoga, part of the knowledge of Brahman, as sung by the Lord in the Upanishad called Bhagavad Gita, ends the sixteenth discourse entitled: The Yoga of Discriminating Between the Divine and Demonic Natures.

Discourse 17

Arjuna asked:
1. Krishna, those men who cast the sacred texts aside,
yet still worship with faith, what is their state?
Do they act from sattva, rajas or tamas?

The Lord responded:
2. Arjuna, the intrinsic faith of men is threefold:
sattvic, rajasa or tamasa. Hear of this from me.
3. Man's faith conforms to his inner nature.
Man is made of faith; whatever the quality
of his faith, that is what he becomes.
4. Men of sattvic nature worship the gods;
men of rajas worship demigods and demons;
those of tamas, ghosts and ghoulish spirits.
5. Men who practise fierce austerities
which are not sanctioned by sacred texts,
who are hypocritical, egotistic,
driven by desires and attachments,
6. who decimate their body's component parts,
and also torture me, dwelling within—
know these possess a demonic nature.
7. Food is also favoured in three kinds,
as are sacrifice, austerity and charity.
Hear from me the distinction between each.
8. Foods promoting longevity, giving energy,
health and happiness, feeding enthusiasm,
which are tasty, rich, nourishing and inviting—
know these to the sattvic type are dear.
9. Foods tart, acidic, salty, very hot, spicy,

	dry, burning, and which cause pain, anguish
	and sickness—these to the rajasa are dear.
10	While soiled foods, tasteless, putrid, stale,
	rejected as impure—these to the tamasa are dear.
11	Sacrifice sanctioned by authority,
	offered duteously, without desire for reward,
	know to be sattvic in character.
12	Best of Bharatas, sacrifice offered for reward,
	in narcissistic show, know as rajasa.
13	While sacrifice not sanctioned by authority,
	circulating no food, lacking sacred hymns,
	which pays no sacrificial fees and is devoid
	of faith, you should know as tamasa.
14	Homage to the gods, Brahmans, gurus
	and the wise, purity, righteousness,
	brahmacharya and non-violence—
	these constitute austerity of the body.
15	Words that are inoffensive, truthful, amiable,
	beneficial, or used when reciting sacred texts—
	these constitute austerity of speech.
16	Serenity, compassion, silence,
	self-restraint and purity of thought—
	these constitute austerity of mind.
17	Arjuna, this three-fold austerity,
	performed by disciplined and faith-filled men
	who do not seek any fruit, is called sattvic.
18	But austerity performed flamboyantly,
	to gain honour, fame or the reverence of others,
	ephemeral and unsound, is termed rajasa.
19	While austerity performed in ignorant
	misunderstanding, torturing oneself
	or harming others, is known as tamasa.
20	Charity given from a sense of duty,
	at the appropriate place and time,
	to the deserving, without seeking reward,
	has been pronounced sattvic.

21 But charity given resentfully,
to win merit, or in expectation
of receiving in return, is called rajasa.

22 While charity given at the wrong time
and place, disdainfully, in bad grace,
to the undeserving, has been declared tamasa.

23 Know "Om Tat Sat" has been pronounced
the three-fold name of Brahman;
from it emanated Brahmans, the Vedas
and sacrifice at the dawn of time.

24 Therefore the savants of Brahman perform
all acts of sacrifice, austerity and charity
in accordance with injunctions of the sacred texts,
beginning each with "Om" on their lips.

25 These seekers of freedom perform
the rituals of sacrifice, austerity and charity,
not seeking rewards, while uttering "Tat".

26 "Sat" is meant in the sense of good and true;
know, Arjuna, "sat" describes auspicious acts too.

27 Consistency in sacrifice, austerity,
and charity is therefore proclaimed "sat",
as is all work performed for this purpose.

28 All sacrifices offered, all gifts of charity,
all austerities that are practised,
if performed without faith, are called "asat".
Know, Arjuna, such acts amount to nothing,
whether performed in this world or the next.

Thus, in the dialogue between Shri Krishna and Arjuna, on the science of Yoga, part of the knowledge of Brahman, as sung by the Lord in the Upanishad called Bhagavad Gita, ends the seventeenth discourse entitled: The Yoga of Identifying the Three Qualities of Faith.

Discourse 18

Arjuna said:
1. Mighty-armed Prince, the demon Kesi's slayer,
inner controller of the entire universe,
I seek to know the truth of sanyasa and tyaga.

The Lord replied:
2. Sanyasa, sages know, involves renunciation
of all action springing from selfish desire;
tyaga, so the wise proclaim, requires
total abandonment of action's fruit.
3. Some thinkers proclaim all action is soiled,
concluding action should be abandoned;
others argue acts of sacrifice, charity,
and austerity should never be given up.
4. Tiger among men, now hear
my conclusion on the issue of tyaga.
Tyaga is said to consist of three types.
5. Actions of sacrifice, austerity
and charity may not be abandoned;
they must be performed, for they purify the wise.
6. Yet, Arjuna, my considered counsel
is that even these acts must be performed
without attachment or desiring action's fruit.
7. It is wrong to renounce one's prescribed duty;
its abandonment through delusion is tamasa.
8. Who abandons his duty due to pain
or fear of physical hardship, will not reap
the benefits of his abandonment, which is rajasa.
9. But when, Arjuna, the allotted task

is performed from a sense of duty,
and both attachment and fruit are abandoned,
that abandonment is called sattvic.

10 Who does not avoid unpleasant work,
nor clings to pleasant action, is an undoubting
one who correctly practises abandonment;
wise, he is fully imbued with sattva.

11 Know none can avoid action; but those who
abandon action's fruit are called tyagi.

12 Action's threefold fruit of agreeable,
disagreeable and mixed accrue after death
to those who do not practise abandonment,
but they never accrue to sanyasis.

13 The teachings of sankhya name five factors
in the accomplishment of all actions:

14 the field, the doer, the instruments,
the various movements, and providence.

15 What man enacts with body, speech or mind,
whether rightly or wrongly, is done via these five.

16 Thus, he who with a clouded intellect
sees the self as the doer in actions,
perversely misunderstanding, he is blind.

17 But he whose intellect is not impure,
and whose motives are not ego driven,
knows he neither slays nor is bound,
though, Arjuna, he slaughters all these here.

18 The knower, knowledge and what is known
comprise action's threefold motivation;
the doer, the action and the organs which act
comprise the threefold aspects of action.

19 In the teachings on the gunas, knowledge,
action and the doer are said to be of three kinds,
according to their natures. Of these now hear.

20 That knowledge by which one imperishable
Being is perceived in all perishable beings,
undivided yet equally divided among all—

know that knowledge to be sattvic.

21 That knowledge by which all beings
are perceived as different entities,
each one separate from all others—
know that knowledge to be rajasa.

22 While that knowledge which irrationally
holds to one aspect, seeing it as the whole,
superficial, and missing the real point—
that knowledge has been declared tamasa.

23 Sattvica action involves doing one's duty,
being performed with no attachments,
without like or dislike, and no desire for fruit.

24 However, rajasa action involves much strain,
being performed egoistically, to quench desire.

25 While tamasa action is performed in ignorance,
by those who disregard the consequences,
their own abilities, and injury or loss.

26 Know that doer is sattvic who is free of ego
and attachment, is committed, perseveres,
and remains unswayed by success or failure.

27 That doer is rajasa who is passionate,
greedy, violent, impure, craves action's fruit,
and is swept by joy and sorrow.

28 While that doer is said to be tamasa
who is undisciplined, uncouth, arrogant,
treats others meanly, is deceitful, lazy,
gets depressed and procrastinates.

29 Now hear me, conqueror of riches,
fully detail the threefold division of intellect
and will, according to their gunas.

30 Arjuna, that intellect is sattvic
which understands the difference between
action and non-action, right and wrong action,
fear and fearlessness, bondage and release.

31 That intellect is rajasa which decides
erroneously between right and wrong,

between what should and should not be done.
32 And that intellect is tamasa which,
trapped in ignorance, thinks right is wrong,
and views everything as upside-down, reversed.
33 That will is sattvic which maintains
yogic harmony between the activities
of mind, vital energies, and the senses.
34 That will is rajasa which, seeking action's fruit,
is attached to wealth, satisfying desires,
and the rewards of acting virtuously.
35 And that will is tamasa which refuses
to abandon somnambulance, anxiety,
fear, depression and self-importance.
36 Now hear of three types of happiness from me.
Know that happiness experienced after
persistent practice, which ends all suffering,
37 which at first tastes like poison but is nectar
in the end, and which is born of the serene
understanding of one's own self, is called sattvic.
38 Happiness felt when the senses interact
with objects, which tastes at first like nectar
but is poison in the end, is termed rajasa.
39 While happiness which stems from laziness,
forgetfulness and somnambulance, deluding
the self from beginning to end, is tamasa.
40 No being on earth, or among the gods
in heaven, can exist free of prakriti's gunas.
41 Thus, scourge of foes, the activities
of Brahmans, Kshatriyas, Vaishyas and Sudras
are defined by their guna qualities.
42 Peacefulness, self-restraint, austerity,
purity, forgiveness, integrity, knowledge
of the manifest and unmanifest, and faith
in religious practices are the Brahman's qualities.
43 Possessing high aspirations, drive,
perseverance, ingenuity, courage in battle,

	generosity, and the ability to govern

generosity, and the ability to govern
denote the Kshatriya's qualities.

44 The Vaishya's qualities consist of trade,
cultivating the earth, and rearing cows;
while service is the Sudra's quality.

45 Each achieves perfection by doing his natural duty.
Now hear how the duteous achieve this.

46 That man achieves perfection whose work
becomes an act of worship, dedicated
to that from which everything emanates,
by which all that exists is pervaded.

47 Better to do one's own work, however humble,
than another's well-performed; for work done
that accords with one's nature incurs no sin.

48 Thus, Arjuna, though it be imperfect,
one's natural work should not be refused;
for as fire is enveloped by smoke,
so are actions clouded by imperfection.

49 But he whose intellect is non-attached,
whose desires are mastered and self subdued
through the practice of renunciation,
attains complete freedom from action.

50 Arjuna, now briefly learn from me
how one who achieves perfection attains
to Brahman, the pinnacle of knowledge.

51 Endowed with a purified intellect,
using will to firmly restrain the self,
detached from sound and other sense objects,
and from the likes and dislikes they engender,

52 living in solitude, eating modestly,
speech, body and mind controlled,
absorbed in meditation, practising vairagya,

53 renouncing ego, violence, pride, desire,
anger and the desire for possessions,
tranquil within and having shed selfishness,
he is eligible for oneness with Brahman.

54 One with Brahman and at peace in himself,
he no longer desires nor grieves;
viewing all equally, he is devoted to me.

55 Through devotion, he experiences my greatness
and the essence of my reality.
Knowing my reality, he merges with me.

56 Whoever makes his refuge none but me,
while still duteously performing his work,
by my grace, gains the everlasting abode.

57 Mentally dedicating all actions to me,
practising the yoga of even-mindedness,
focus your thought exclusively on me.

58 Your thought thus concentrated on me,
my grace will ensure you conquer all obstacles.
But if ego stops you hearing, you are lost.

59 If, ego driven, you think, "I shall not fight",
that resolve is futile; your nature will force you to.

60 That action, which deluded you would not do,
Arjuna, you yet shall do, bound as you are
by the duty born of your innate nature.

61 Ishvara, residing in the hearts of all,
by his maya causes all to revolve, as if on a wheel.

62 Bharata, seek refuge in him with all
your being; by his grace you will attain
to the eternal abode of supreme peace.

63 Thus, I have revealed this hidden knowledge to you.
Ponder it carefully, then act as you choose.

64 But first hear again my sublime secret,
the deepest secret of all; you are so dear
to me, I offer this teaching for your good.

65 Fix your mind on me; give your heart to me;
prostrate and offer your sacrifice to me.
I promise, you will then come to me,
for you are especially dear to me.

66 Abandoning religious laws, take refuge in me.
I shall release you from sin. Do not fear!

67   Never impart this to he who lacks
austerity, devotion, or a desire to hear,
and particularly not to he who scorns me.

68   But he who, out of his great love for me,
shares this secret knowledge with my devotees,
will assuredly enter into me.

69   None does better service among men than he;
none on earth is dearer to me than he.

70   And whoever studies this sacred dialogue,
know that through the sacrifice of knowledge
he worships me. This I fervently believe.

71   That faith-filled undoubting seeker who
absorbs these words also shall be released;
he will gain the happy worlds of the virtuous.

72   Arjuna, have you heard this with a focused mind?
Tell me, conqueror of riches, has your delusion,
born of ignorance, been totally dispersed?

Arjuna replied:
73   Infallible Lord, by your divine grace
my delusion is destroyed, understanding gained.
Devoid now of doubt, I shall do your bidding.

Sanjaya said:
74   Thus I witnessed this marvellous, mind-tingling
dialogue between Vasudeva and mahatma Arjuna.

75   By Vyasa's favour, before my very eyes,
I heard the secret yoga spoken to Arjuna
by Krishna himself, the master of yoga.

76   My King, each time I recall that sublime
discourse of Kesheva and Arjuna,
my thrilled heart surges with joy;

77   and remembering too that breath-taking form
Shri Krishna adopted, my wonder abounds,
and I exult over and over again.

78   Wherever is Krishna, lord of yoga,

and wherever Arjuna, the great bowman,
good fortune, prosperity, righteousness
and victory are there. This is my conviction.

Thus, in the dialogue between Shri Krishna and Arjuna, on the science of Yoga, part of the knowledge of Brahman, as sung by the Lord in the Upanishad called Bhagavad Gita, ends the eighteenth discourse entitled: The Yoga of Liberation Through Renunciation.

Appendices

The philosophic background

In order to appreciate the *Bhagavad Gita*'s philosophy, the reader requires some knowledge of the Sankhya system which forms a conceptual framework on which poem's thought is built.

The Sankhya system provides one of the central strands of Indian spiritual thought. Its founding is traditionally ascribed to Kapila, an ascetic about whom nothing otherwise is known. Interestingly he, or whoever thought out the system, has no place for God as the creator of the cosmos. Instead, two fundamental principles are posited, purusha (primordial spirit) and prakriti (primordial matter). Both purusha and prakriti are eternal and unmanifest. Prakriti contains three constituent parts, called gunas. In the beginning these three gunas were in equilibrium. But on being disturbed by the presence of purusha disequilibrium came about and prakriti, through the gunas, manifested the universe. This resultant manifestation may be best indicated diagrammatically. [See the next page.]

First came prakriti's will (buddhi) to manifest itself. Then, as a result of this will, came individuation (ahamkara) whereby prakriti broke up into various separate entities. These entities were divided into two worlds, organic and inorganic. The organic world consists of mind (manas), the five senses of perception (hearing, sight, touch, taste and smell), and the five organs of action (the hands, the feet, the tongue and the two organs of excretion). The inorganic world consists of the five subtle elements (sound, form, touch, savour and smell), and the five gross elements (ether, wind, fire, water and earth).

This is the Sankhya system in its cosmological form. But the system also provides a schema which explains how human beings function in the world. Thus the senses perceive the world,

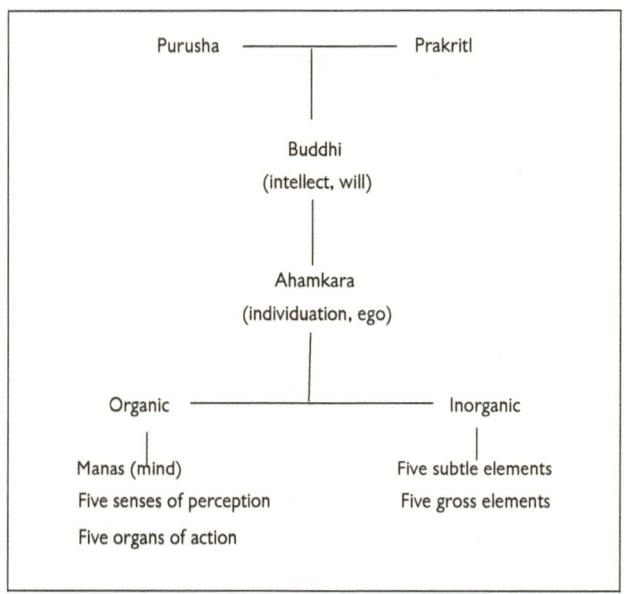

then pass those perceptions on to the mind. The mind in turn processes and organises the senses' perceptions into information which is passed through the ego to the intellect. The intellect, on the basis of this information, decides what is to be done and, by its will, that decision is relayed via the ego back to the mind which has the decision executed by the organs of action. It can be seen, therefore, that in the Sankhya system the cosmological macrocosm is reflected in the human microcosm.

THE GITA'S DIVERGENCE FROM THE SANKHYA SYSTEM

The *Bhagavad Gita* accepts all the demarcations of manifest prakriti indicated above. What it does not accept is the Sankhya system's concept of the relationship between purusha and prakriti. For the Sankhya philosopher prakriti manifests the universe and all its multiple forms, and purusha divides itself to give each particular form an individual spirit. The two principles are thus equal but separate, working harmoniously, but intrinsically independent. This is not the *Bhagavad Gita's* view.

The *Bhagavad Gita's* concept is that purusha is identical with Brahman (God), and that unmanifest prakriti is a part of Brahman, being the cosmic seed which Brahman manifests as the universe. Thus the purusha existing within each form is a particle of Brahman itself. The universe, and all the creatures in it, are therefore manifestations of Brahman, are sustained by Brahman, and return to Brahman when the cycle of cosmic manifestation is complete. Hence nothing exists but Brahman, which simultaneously transcends, pervades and manifests as the universe.

The purusha in each form is termed atman (self). Just as Brahman transcends the universe, so atman transcends the body it dwells within, existing before that body was born, and continuing to exist after that body dies. It is by knowing atman that human beings may know Brahman. The reason atman knows neither Brahman nor itself is that it becomes attached to and identified first with the body and then, through the body's senses, with various sense-objects existing in the world.

Another name for the universe is maya (illusion). Maya is Brahman revealed as manifest prakriti. But maya at the same time hides Brahman in its unmanifest, transcendent aspect. This is because human beings, attached to the body and sense-objects, become lost in the vast variety of manifest maya and remain ignorant of the unmanifest within and behind that manifestation. The atman which is attached to maya, and therefore exists in a state of ignorance regarding itself, does not pass on to Brahman at the death of the body in which it dwells, but instead is reborn in another body. Thus is perpetrated the cycle of birth, death and rebirth. What keeps atman bound to this cycle is karma resulting from the activities of the three gunas.

KARMA AND THE THREE GUNAS

The three gunas are strands of prakriti. By name they are sattva, rajas and tamas. "Sat" means intelligence, "raja" means king, and "tam" is darkness. Because the cosmos is prakriti's manifestation, and the gunas are prakriti's essential substance, these three permeate everything in the cosmos. On the cosmological level, sattva may be seen as cosmic laws, rajas as energy and matter, and tamas as inertia. On the human level, sattva is happiness and knowledge, rajas is restlessness and passion, and tamas is ignorance and sleep.

When the three gunas interact work is done. This work is called karma. All karma binds atman to the body. Sattva binds through happiness and knowledge, rajas through restlessness and passion, tamas through ignorance and sleep. If atman is bound to the body by karma it is not released from the cycle of birth and death when that body dies, but instead is reborn into another body. This cycle of rebirth is not broken by performing any particular work, but by transcending the realm of the three gunas and karma altogether. When transcendence is achieved atman realizes its nature and at death goes to the spiritual realm, no longer subject to the cycle of rebirth.

The chief metaphysical implication arising from this is that a person who engages in "good" deeds no more escapes the rounds of births and deaths than someone who does "bad." Both are performing actions, therefore karma is being produced. And all karma, whether good or bad, binds atman to the body.

So why should we act at all? The *Bhagavad Gita's* answer to this question is that because we have a body subject to the gunas we must of necessity act. If we do not act the body is not maintained, and it dies. But all action is performed only via the three gunas, therefore whatever we do will be permeated by either sattva, raja or tamas. Spiritually sattva leads to purity, rajas to impurity, and tamas to perversity. So, as regards the seeker's spiritual development, sattvic action is to be preferred.

Yet in the final analysis even the purity, knowledge, goodness and happiness of sattva has to be transcended if the quest for release is to be fulfilled. How does one transcend sattva, rajas and tamas? The *Bhagavad Gita's* answer is that the seeker does so through the practice of yoga.

THE FOUR YOGAS

Yoga literally means "plus." In the widest sense, that which takes one towards Brahman—being plus—is yoga, and that which takes one away is contrary to yoga. Thus yoga is any path, any attitude, any practice which takes one towards Brahman, or, translating into Western theological terms, God. Each of the *Bhagavad Gita's* eighteen discourses are considered to indicate a path towards Brahman/God, therefore each is termed a yoga. There are many different forms of yoga in Vedic teachings, but the *Bhagavad Gita* primarily emphasises jnanayoga, karmayoga, bhaktiyoga and dhyanayoga.

Jnanayoga is the path of knowledge and is practised by sankhyas (not to be confused with the Sankhya system). The disquisition on the immortality of atman in Discourse Two forms the introduction to jnanayoga, which has as its basic premise that our spiritual self (atman) is not identical with the body. The knowledge jnanayoga seeks is direct, experiential knowledge of unmanifest atman. However, to achieve this the sankhya has to transcend the three gunas, so in order to do so knowledge of the manifest world and its activities is also required. But knowledge of the manifest world is sought only insofar as it assists transcendence. Essentially, jnanayoga is concerned with the task of establishing and sustaining consciousness in the unmanifest realm of atman and Brahman.

Karmayoga is the path of action. It is, according to the *Bhagavad Gita*, the most effective method of achieving self and God-realisation. But if all action binds atman to the body, how can practising karmayoga, and therefore acting, enable atman to achieve release? The *Bhagavad Gita's* answer to this apparent contradiction is that all action binds save that action performed with an attitude of selfless service. To do this one has to be non-attached while acting and surrender the fruit of all action to God.

The reasoning that justifies this concept is that Brahman exists beyond the actions of the three gunas. Therefore Brahman does not act. Only the three gunas act. Further, while Brahman has manifested and sustains the cosmos, it is not attached to anything it has manifested, and therefore is neither bound nor stained by the karma which results from whatever action occurs. Similarly, within human beings, atman does not act. Rather the three gunas in the body act. Hence being established in atman means the three gunas are transcended and the self is not stained by the karma which necessarily arises out of action.

Accordingly, to become established in atman karmayoga advocates two principle practices: being non-attached while acting, and not seeking the fruit of action. Instead, the fruit action is surrendered to Brahman/God. The karmayogi's actions then become acts of selfless service. To achieve this, the karmayogi allows the gunas to perform the action, while he or she abides in non-acting atman. Abiding in non-action, karma is no longer accrued. And so the rounds of births and deaths are escaped.

Bhaktiyoga is the path of devotion. Its aim is to constantly worship Brahman in one form or another. This form presents a personalized form of Brahman by which worshippers may worship the formless, unconditioned Brahman that exists "behind" it. In the *Bhagavad Gita* this form is presented by Krishna, who appears to be a man, but is really a manifestation of the Absolute. The highest form of worship is silent, inner remembrance. God is unmanifest and therefore formless, but in order to remember and worship God most people prefer a form by which the formless may be visualised. For those bhaktas Discourse Eleven contains a famed passage which shows Krishna in the form of God's destructive aspect.

Underpinning all three yogas is dhyanayoga (meditation). the aim of which is experience atman, and therefore Brahman, directly. The method of meditation leading to atman's realisation is succinctly described in Discourse Six. Obviously dhyanayoga is essential to the practice of jnanayoga, because it provides a form of practice for living constantly in the unmanifest. However, it also helps karmayogis and bhaktas appreciate atman within.

As to which of the three paths is preferred, the *Bhagavad Gita* recommends karmayoga. It is easy to practise and direct in its result. Of course elements of each path creep into the practice of the others. For example, the karmayogi needs knowledge if he or she is to act correctly. Just as the surgeon operating without knowledge of anatomy will kill rather than cure, so action performed without knowledge is unlikely to lead to a positive result. Similarly, the sankhya practising meditation needs to apply to it the principles of karmayoga, for meditation is work, and if the aim of meditation is to be achieved it needs to be performed in a non-attached manner, without seeking rewards. And the bhakta needs jnanayoga's knowledge of the unmanifest in order to transcend form during worship, and also karmayoga's teaching on the attitude to maintain while engaged in that worship. The *Bhagavad Gita's* view is that jnanayoga's approach of holding fast to the unmanifest is difficult to sustain while living in the body, while bhaktas tend to remain attached to their chosen form and find it difficult to appreciate the formless beyond the form. Thus karmayoga, easy and direct, is the recommended path.

It is in this recommendation that the *Bhagavad Gita* is of great relevance to today's seekers. The majority today live as householders, working and raising families. Thus we live in the realm of action. Karmayoga being the pre-eminent philosophy of action, it offers a way for the seeker to realize the self and Brahman while engaged in action.

SACRIFICE AND SERVICE

No form of yoga will lead to realisation without being complemented by yajna. In this version of the *Bhagavad Gita* yajna has been rendered either as either "sacrifice" or "service", depending on context. Conceptually, yajna involves both. Those who seek realisation have to serve a teaching by doing what it requires. At the lowest level this means sacrificing various bodily pleasures and desires; at the highest it means sacrificing our sense of self. Just as parents sacrifice much to nurture their children, serving their requirements and needs, so must the seeker sacrifice a great deal to nurture an engagement with atman, serving its requirements and needs. And the more our sense in inner self blossoms, the more we have to offer in service to others. Thus sacrifice and service go hand in hand.

The *Bhagavad Gita* recognises that there are many forms of sacrifice, but all take the seeker to the same goal of realisation. In jnanayoga the seeker engages in knowledge sacrifice, by which the ego is sacrificed in atman. In karmayoga the seeker engages in work sacrifice, by which the fruits of all work are sacrificed to Brahman/God. In bhaktiyoga the seeker engages in worship sacrifice, by which the attachments of body, heart and mind are sacrificed in constant remembrance of Brahman/God. And in dhyanayoga the seeker's sacrifice is of the manifest world in the unmanifest spiritual realm.

However, different people have different abilities and capacities. Thus what one person has to sacrifice will not be what another has to sacrifice. And neither will all seekers serve, know or worship in the same way or to the same extent. It is in acknowledgment of these differences that the *Bhagavad Gita* brings in its teaching on the castes.

CASTE DIVISIONS

The *Bhagavad Gita* identifies four castes: brahman, kshatriya, vaishya and sudra. Every human being is a member of one of these four. Traditionally one becomes a member of a particular caste as a result of birth, taking on the caste of one's parents. In the view of Shri Muniji, when the notion of caste is approached ignorantly it results in exploitation, suppression and injustice. In his view caste needs to be understood in a spiritual sense. The following is Shri Muniji's teaching on caste.

From the spiritual perspective one becomes a member of a caste not through birth, but according to one's innate nature. Thus the caste system is not an indication of status, or lack of it, but of inner nature and type. The work each person is drawn towards varies according to his or her type. The brahman engages in intellectual work, the kshatriya is a leader and organiser, the vaishya is the agricultural and industrial worker, and the sudra works in the service industries that maintain the others. To give an example: the inventor of a new device, having spent much thought during its invention, is a brahman; the kshatriyas are the businessmen and women who organise its manufacture and distribution; the vaishyas are those who build it; and the sudras perform those services necessary to keep all running.

Ideally, each person should fulfil his or her function out of a sense of duty, not from a desire to exploit the situation for profit or power. By doing work which accords with innate type not only is the society maintained, but that work, conscientiously and wisely performed, becomes the means by which karmayoga may be practised. Thus what matters ultimately is not how grandiose or humble the work is that we do, but whether or not it is used as a means by which to attain spiritual realization and release from the cycle of births and deaths. Work done in a spirit of non-attachment, without seeking rewards, will take one towards realisation. Work done from selfish desire, to acquire wealth, status, privilege and possessions, will not. For when the body dies it is not the work one did which counts, but whether or not one is established in atman.

REALISATION AND THE MOMENT OF DEATH

The *Bhagavad Gita* considers the moment of death to be of crucial importance. Its view is that whatever one's chief preoccupation during life, whatever one's principal attachment, one's thoughts will return to at the moment of death. Only if Brahman is remembered at the moment of death will the seeker go to Brahman. But to remember Brahman at the moment of death means that remembrance of Brahman has been sustained during one's life, while to remember Brahman requires being established in atman. Thus it is through being established in atman that Brahman will be attained, and the cycle of births and deaths escaped. The trick is that, because death may come at any moment, remembrance needs to be continuous.

The obtaining of release cannot, therefore, be likened to the Christian death-bed confession, whereby the dying person attempts a last-minute reprieve from his or her sins. If the realm of action is not transcended before death, it will not be transcended after death.

Indeed, the *Bhagavad Gita* staes in several places that ordinary religious practices are quite insufficient to obtain release. Religious rituals are performed in the realm of the three gunas, and cannot take the worshipper beyond that realm. Therefore religious rituals, and religion itself, must be abandoned and experiential knowledge of atman and Brahman sought. Only by transcending religion will the goal of knowledge and liberation be achieved.

CONCLUSION

After hearing all this (and much else which this brief summary has not touched on), Arjuna realises his foolishness in not acting, and declares that he will now do his duty and fight with, and against, his kinsmen. So what is the battle he is to engage in? Clearly, it is not just an historical battle that requires the death of his cousins. Rather, at heart it is the battle for the self.

To offer an allegorical reading, the field of Kuru on which the battle takes place is life. The two opposing armies are those forces that take the seeker either towards or away from Brahman/God and atman/self. Arrayed within the body they are manifestations of consciousness itself. Arjuna is the questing spirit which seeks release. Krishna is the voice of the teaching which guides him. And the kinsmen who must die are those various parts within which are limiting in their nature and must be given up if the fullness of realisation is to be achieved.

Notes on discourses

The *Bhagavad Gita* draws together diverse strands of Indian mystical thought and practice. Over the centuries scholars have disentangled the strands to better understand how they were woven together. The central strands of thought include:

- the metaphysical perspective of Sankhya philosophy;
- traditional religious beliefs expressed in the myths recorded in the Vedas;
- the concepts of karma and of escape from the cycle of rebirth;
- the identity of atman (self) with Brahman (God as Absolute);
- yogic practices which provide the foundations for Indian mysticism.

What makes the *Bhagavad Gita* unique is the way its writers have combined these strands into a coherent spiritual and metaphysical outlook. Conversely, the diversity of sources also results in divergent, even contradictory, perspectives. For example, some verses (17:24) state that worshippers need to act according to the religious injunctions of the Vedas, while others (2:42-46) assert that the wise have no use for religious worship. In some verses (18:45) the poem advocates for the caste system, saying caste duties need to be carried out; elsewhere (9:20-21) it says that attachment to religion, caste and social differences stop seekers from becoming wise. Most of the poem is written from a warrior perspective, however the last three discourses emphasise priestly practices and outlook. Throughout, the poem presents Krishna as a form of God to be worshipped, yet it is equally firm all forms must be transcended.

Naturally, these multiple conceptual strands have led to the poem being interpreted from a wide variety of perspectives. Yogis, religious worshippers, Sanskrit scholars, philosophers, ascetics, literary critics and readers who know little about Indian spirituality, each find material in the poem that supports their outlook. Hence while Gandhi drew inspiration from the *Bhagavad Gita* when he constructed his political strategy of non-violent resistance, the poem eulogises the warrior approach to life and ends with Krishna exhorting Arjuna to enter the battle and kill his kinsmen.

This demonstrates there can be no single definitive interpretation of the *Bhagavad Gita*. It is a kaleidoscope that changes according to the angle from which it is viewed. Indeed, thoughtful readers will find that with successive readings, and as their own experience and understanding develops, some aspects of the poem come into prominence while other portions previously as significant fall away. The complexities of the text, and the subtleties of its thought, require the reader to approach it creatively, projecting themselves and their own spiritual search into the poem in order to extract the most from it.

The following notes are offered with two primary aims. One is to explain the poem's religious, mythological and historical references. The other is to draw attention to key spiritual concepts. My notes are a modest contribution to the vast volume that has been written about the *Bhagavad Gita*, Non-technical, they are primarily designed to provide an entrance into the text for those who are unfamiliar with Vedic mythology and Indian philosophy.

DISCOURSE ONE

The literary purpose of the first discourse is to take the reader from the story-telling mode of the *Mahabharata* and into the poem's abstract, philosophic mode. Some scholars consider that the poem's style indicates the *Bhagavad Gita* was added to the *Mahabharata* after the larger work was completed. Conversely, others maintain both were written at the same time.

Dramatically, the first discourse introduces the warriors lined up to do battle. It then swiftly moves on to focus on Arjuna.

Arjuna's problem is that despite being a warrior, and despite it being his duty to fight, he cannot help but consider the death and destruction the battle will bring about. This thinking leads him to declare to Krishna that, no matter how right his cause, he will not fight. Arjuna's moral dilemma presents Krishna with the opportunity to present a wide-ranging philosophical and spiritual discussion regarding duty, action, whether or not the self actually dies, and the nature of Brahman which underpins all reality.

Comments on particular verses follow. A point to note is that Krishna exhorts Arjuna to fight on the grounds that all the warriors he is worried about are already dead. In the following I have described their future deaths to illustrate Krishna's assertion.

1. The battle took place on the field of Kuru, which was situated in what is now East Punjab, north of Delhi. The field is named after King Kuru, common ancestor of both families, whose home it was. The field is sacred because of the austerities he and others performed there.

2. Drona taught the arts of war, and particularly archery, to both sets of cousins. During the battle that is to follow he heard a report that his son had died. He immediately sat down and entered a state of meditation. While doing so Dhirstadyumna killed him by cutting off his head. Moreover, the report of his son's death was false.

3. Dhirstadyumna was commander-in-chief of the Pandu's army. Before he was born his father, Drupada, offered a sacrifice, seeking a son to slay his hated enemy, Drona. Dhirstadyumna is that son. Clever, he tricked Drona into teaching him how to become a great warrior. He later used those skills to kill Drona.

4. Arjuna and Bhima were the third and second oldest of the Pandu brothers. Their mother was Kunti. Satyaki was a disciple of Arjuna. He survived the Mahabharata war, but died in an inter-tribal skirmish soon after. Virata gave the Pandus refuge during their year of incognito existence within the kingdom. He and his three sons died in the war. Maharatha was the highest military title. Myth says such a warrior

can fight 10,000 warriors single-handedly. Drupada was the father of Dhirstadyumna and sworn enemy of Drona, who killed him during the war.

5   Dhrishtaketu, the king of the Chedis, was killed by Drona. Chekitana was a maharatha and commander of a one-seventh section of the Pandu's army. Kasiraja was a hero and a maharatha. Purujit was uncle to the three oldest Pandu brothers. Saibya was the father-in-law of Yudhishthira.

6   Yudhmanyu and Uttamaujas were brothers who guarded the wheels of Arjuna's chariot during battle. They were killed by Ashwatthama one night, as they slept. Subhadra was Arjuna's second wife, sister to Krishna. Draupadi was the daughter of Drupada, sister of Dhirstadyumna, and common wife of the five Pandus, by each of whom she had one son. All these sons were killed by Ashwatthama as they slept.

8   Bhishma was Krishna's brother and commander-in-chief of Duryodhana's army. While young he undertook a vow of celibacy in order to enable his father to marry. Mortally wounded during the Mahabharata war, he lay on a bed of arrows for eighty-three days, waiting for a propitious time to die. Karna was Kunti's son, conceived by the sun god. After Drona's death Karna became commander-in-chief of Duryodhana's army. This role lasted just two days, ending when Arjuna killed him. Kripa was brother-in-law of Drona. He was proficient in the Vedas and a master of archery. Myth says he not only survived the war, but is still alive today. Ashwatthama was Drona's son. He was a maharatha whom legend says is also still living. Bhurishava was a maharatha killed by Satyaki. Vikarna was a maharatha and one of Dhritarastra's one hundred sons. Some commentators consider that the participation of all these warriors indicates this was not a local war, but involved all India. Others argue it was indeed a regional war, as demonstrated by the fact two branches of one family were responsible for the war occurring at all.

11 *But guard Bhishma, for then will be no surprises.* Drupada's son, Shikhandhi, had been born female, but was later transformed

into a male. However, Bhishma regarded him as still female, and so had vowed never to fight him. Here Duryodhana is warning his men to ensure Shikhandhi does not inadvertently appear in front of Bhishma during battle and challenge him to combat, because it would have disastrous consequences.

16 Nakula and Sahadeva were the fourth and fifth sons of Pandu, by his second wife, Madri.

17 For Shikhandhi see the note on verse 11.

20 Hanuman was a famed monkey-devotee, an embodiment of dedicated service, purity and valour. His image was on Arjuna's banner.

21 Achyuta is a name for Krishna. It means "one who stands firm".

30 Gandiva was Arjuna's bow, given him by the god, Indra.

32 Govinda is an epithet for Krishna, meaning "one who has mastered the five senses".

35 The three worlds are heaven, earth and the underworld.

40 In verses 40 to 44 Arjuna presents a reason for not fighting his extended family. He argues that families propagate traditional virtues, so killing his own family members would destroy those virtues; without virtues their women will become corrupted; and with women's corruption comes the non-performance of ancestral worship, followed by the destruction of the social structure. This is the literal traditional interpretation. Shri Muniji's spiritual interpretation is that the castes are our various inner parts. Virtuous actions keep our inner parts in balance, evil actions make them unbalanced. Blood is thought. Age-old traditions represent the spiritual knowledge passed from teacher to pupil; offerings to deceased ancestors represent what we give back to those who went before us and whose teachings guide and inspire us today; and hell is an existence in which thought is uncontrolled and the inner parts exist in a chaotic, destructive relationship. When spiritual knowledge is no longer passed on the individual spirit becomes tainted and is reborn into another similarly chaotic body.

DISCOURSE TWO

Krishna initially responds to Arjuna's statement that he will not fight by appealing to his sense of warrior manliness. In verses 4 to 8 Arjuna responds, justifying why he refuses to kill his kinsmen. In answer Krishna introduces the two forms of yoga fundamental to the Gita's teaching: jnanayoga, the path of knowledge, and karmayoga, the path of action. The concepts and technical language regarding jnanayoga are drawn from the *Upanishads*. By contrast, karmayoga is introduced here for the first time in Indian spirituality. It is Krishna's discourse on these two forms of yoga that offers the knowledge which provides this discourse's title, *The Yoga of Knowledge*.

It is interesting that all this philosophic discussion occurs not in the context of the lives of priests, but in the context of the warrior's outlook. Krishna begins by discussing the warrior's need to act honourably and dutifully, and to embrace righteous war because it is the proper activity of warriors. The question is, how can Arjuna fulfil his duty by entering battle philosophically, fearing death for neither himself nor for those he is about to kill? In a culture where engaging in action is a social norm, there is a need for a spiritual philosophy of action. Karmayoga answers this need. Because it builds on the principles of jnanayoga, jnanayoga is introduced in verses 12 to 39. From verse 40 the application of these principles to karmayoga is outlined.

12   This verse introduces the idea that the spiritual self transcends the physical realm. In doing so, it references *Katha Upanishad* 2:18: "The Self that knows is not born, does not die; it sprang from nothing, nothing sprang from it. The Ancient [Self] is unborn, eternal, everlasting; he does not die, though the body dies." The aim of jnanayoga is the acquisition of knowledge of this non-dying self. (The quotations from the *Upanishads*, here and following, come from Max Müller's translation. His language has been adjusted to match contemporary usage.)

19   This verse uses the same language as *Katha* 2:19: "If the killer

thinks that he kills, if the killed thinks he is killed, they do not understand; for this does not kill, nor is that one killed." The similarity further reinforces the idea that the *Katha Upanishad* is the source of the expressions used here.

31   Having expounded, in the previous verses, the idea of the spiritual self as unborn, undying and transcendent, Krishna now brings the argument back to Arjuna, arguing that he needs to fulfil his duty as a warrior by fighting. This emphasis on action, and doing one's duty, leads naturally to a consideration of karmayoga.

40   The fundamentals of karmayoga are presented from verses 40 to 53. These include: the need to control the intellect; casting off the religious teachings of the Vedas, including the desire to reach heaven; rising above the activity of the gunas; renouncing attachments and the fruits of action; disengaging from the opposites; and sustaining concentrated awareness of atman within. These teachings are expanded in later discourses; for now, the conceptual ground of karmayoga is laid.

41   *In this, Arjuna, the intellect is one-pointed.* According to the Sankhya psychospiritual system, the intellect is not the same as the mind. Intellect is associated with will and directs the mind. The intellect thinks and discerns, and so is aligned with the active ego and spiritual self, whereas the mind is a passive receptacle for thoughts and so tends to be captured by, and to reflect, sense experience. Alternatively, purifying the mind allows the intellect to flow through it.

42   The Vedas are the oldest Indian spiritual writings. Four in number, they primarily record religious myths, rituals and worship, although some parts present mystical and philosophic teachings, particularly certain hymns and the *Upanishads*. A long-standing tradition is that the Vedas existed in oral form for thousands of years before they were eventually written down by Vyasa's pupils, at his instigation.

Arjuna, the ignorant delight in the Vedas' letter. That shallow attachment to the Vedas as insufficient for those who seek spiritual engagement is also stated in *Katha Upanishad*

2:23: "The Self cannot be gained by [studying] the Vedas, nor by understanding, nor by much learning." The spiritual teaching based on the *Upanishads* later came to be known as Vedanta, literally, the end of the Vedas. That is, Vedanta is realised when the myths, rituals and teachings of the Vedas are transcended and that which gave birth to the Vedas is known. Whether the verses contain a a subtext of derision for priestly brahmans and their rituals is open to debate. Certainly, verses 42 to 44 may be read as a criticism of Vedic ritual, which is seen as being spiritually limited.

45 *The three gunas are the Vedas' domain.* Here metaphysical aspects of Sankhya philosophy are introduced. As a further comment on those attached to Vedic ritual, the writer situates ritualistic religious practices in the realm of the three gunas. This idea is taken no further here, but is dealt with extensively in the following discourse.

46 This is an interesting verse because it reads like a second thought. Either the writer thought his criticism of the priestly outlook had gone too far and he wanted to correct the extremity of his argument by adding that the brahman who knows does indeed transcend limiting, fruit-seeking religious ritual and so arrive at true knowledge, or this verse is a later interpolation made by a defender of brahmanic practices. However, the end result is the same, with the verse indicating that knowledge is achieved through inwardly directed action, not action that is entirely outwardly directed. In all this it appears that one of the writer's strategies in verses 41 to 46 is to introduce a number of philosophic concepts, so laying the seeds for ideas to be developed in the following discourses.

48 The yoga referred to in this verse is karmayoga. Yoga is defined here as requiring the seeker to be non-attached during the performance of any action and not seek the fruit of action, instead remaining even-minded in success and failure. This enables the yogi to maintain inner equanimity, a state identified as the essence of karmayoga.

51 One of the spiritual goals proposed by the *Bhagavad Gita*

is that of an individual's release from the rounds of births and deaths. This is also the goal of all Hindu metaphysical systems, as well as of Jainism and Buddhism. All the verses from 42 to here make the point that those practising Vedic religious rituals (or any religious ritual) ostensibly do so in order with the aim of reaching heaven, but they only achieve rebirth. The real spiritual goal is the liberated blissful state of release from the cycle of births and deaths.

53 This introduction to the goal of spirituality ends with a statement about the need for the karmayogi to control the mind, and not allow it to become diverted by irrelevant issues. With the intellect focused and not distracted the yogi is able to remain focused on atman within.

54 *Samadhi* literally means concentration. It is a heightened state that results from one-pointed focus when awareness is directed back onto itself. With karmayoga introduced, and the process of steadfast concentration identified as a key to spiritual realisation, the writer next has Arjuna ask, on the reader's behalf, for a fuller explanation of what is involved.

The remainder of the discourse answers the question Arjuna asked in verse 54. In the introduction to jnanayoga Krishna described the nature of atman. In verses 55 to 71 he describes how a seeker may experience atman while living in the body, engaged in action. The linking of jnanayoga and karmayoga show that both are required in order to apprehend the spiritual and achieve its realisation. Thus jnanayoga provides a metaphysical understanding of the goal which is to be achieved, while karmayoga indicates how the experience of atman may be pragmatically realised.

Throughout these verses a number of themes are introduced that are repeated throughout the poem: remaining non-attached to sense objects; controlling thinking; eschewing the opposites of pain and pleasure, joy and sorrow; finding satisfaction in the inner spiritual self; remaining inwardly centred and in peace; and renouncing ego and desires. Note, however, that in none of this is action itself to be renounced. Rather, the point is that by practising karmayoga, and by living in accordance with the spiritual philosophy of jnanayoga, the seeker may achieve the goal of spirituality while continuing to perform an active role in the world. In all that is stated in these verses, equanimity remains a key inner state that needs to be achieved.

72 *Brahman-nirvana.* Brahman is God as the Absolute. Nirvana is spiritual happiness, in which deep peace is experienced. Thus this term refers to the highest state of union with Brahman.

DISCOURSE THREE

The second discourse introduces the theme of knowledge and shows how jnanayoga reveals true knowledge, while karmayoga is founded on knowledge revealed by jnanayoga, its practice taking the seeker towards knowledge. This third discourse focuses on the way to turn action into a spiritual practice, thus the title, *The Yoga of Karma.* From verse 36 it also comments on the cause of evil action.

Fundamental to the discussion is that action cannot be avoided. We live in the world, and the world is kept functioning by action, therefore we have to engage in action. The discourse argues that there are two fundamental kinds of action: action performed for self-interested reward, and action performed as service eith an attitude of sacrifice. Action becomes service when we realise that the realm of action is a cycle in which we must necessarily take part while not being attached to either the fruit or results of our actions. Thus we don't act because we want things to go our way; rather, we act because that is required of us by the situation we are in and the social role we have to play. Action then becomes sacrifice, because we are consciously contributing to the cycle of action rather than just taking from it or trying to avoid it. As verse 16 states: *Who doesn't keep the wheel turning, Arjuna, which thus rolls through this world, sinful, sense-sated, lives his life in vain.*

Non-attachment during the performance of action, and not desiring to possess the results of action, are two ideas that are repeated throughout the poem. The way to remain non-attached is not to avoid acting. Instead, it is achieved by attaching oneself to atman each moment of acting. The psychospiritual system of Sankhya philosophy is used to help clarify how this is done. Sankhya identifies, in descending order, atman, ego, intellect, mind, the organs of actions, the senses and sense objects. These form a chain which links the spiritual realm to the physical world, and enables atman to perceive, process perceptions, and respond.

According to the *Bhagavad Gita's* interpretation of Sankhya philosophy, purusha (primordial spirit) generated prakriti (primordial matter). The latter consists of the three gunas of sattva (light), rajas (energy) and tamas (enervation). As jiva, creatures consisting of spirit and matter, we do not act. Instead it is the three gunas, acting on each other, that produce activity in the world. In contrast, our personal atman, being a portion of spiritual purusha, transcends material prakriti and its three gunas. Therefore the way to engage in action as a spiritual practice is to remain centred in atman while engaging at the level of the three gunas. In this discourse the argument is made that the spiritual essence of action is doing one's duty while remaining focused on atman. Then one's actions will be spiritualised, simultaneously becoming an act of service and sacrifice.

A final comment is that in verses 22, 23 and 24 Krishna introduces himself as a personification of transcendent Brahman, establishing a notion that is developed in the following discourses.

1   This discourse begins with Arjuna asking a question that was presumably current when it was written. Other questions are posed in the following discourses. This particular question centres on whether knowledge or action should be preferred spiritually. More plainly, should a seeker withdraw from worldly life to develop spiritual perceptions or continue to engage in worldly activity?

3   Sankhyas are those who practise jnanayoga. The relationship between jnanayoga and karmayoga, introduced in the previous discourse, is now taken to a deeper level.

4   Beginning with this verse, and through to verse 35, a complex answer is developed to Arjuna's question. The answer begins with the assertion that we can't achieve freedom from action

by refusing to act, nor can we gain knowledge merely by passively ceasing to act. Verse 5 states that because we live in the material world, because the material world is governed by the gunas, and because our organs of action are part of the gunas, we cannot avoid acting.

6   The previous two verses examined the impossibility of not acting from a metaphysical perspective. This verse and the next answer the question from a psychological perspective.

9   *Humanity is bound by all action save that action performed as sacrifice.* The word translated here as sacrifice is, in the original Sanskrit, *yajna*. Yajna can also be translated as service. It involves both. A complex argument regarding the virtue of sacrifice is now developed. This argument, which ends at verse 15, is an excellent example of the way the writer synthesises various strands of Indian thought into a harmonious whole.

14 This and the next verse present the idea that everything in the entire cycle of existence emanates from Brahman.

15 Scholars do not agree on how best to interpret this verse. The problem arises because Brahman is used twice; the first time to indicate the material realm which gives rise to action, and the second time to indicate the transcendent immaterial source of the material realm. As the first is the realm of prakriti, I have used the term prakriti instead of Brahman in the first instance.

16 This verse concludes the discussion on sacrifice by reiterating what was stated in verses 4 and 5, but this time from a subjective perspective, from within human experience.

17 In keeping with the thought of the *Upanishads*, atman is now linked to Brahman, and transcendence of the realm of action is described in metaphysical terms. Note that while the verse states that *such a one has no action to perform*, this does not mean that action should be avoided. Verse 18 explains what is meant. Such a one has no action to perform because he or she has no personal biases and is not motivated by self-interest.

20 Janaka was the philosopher-king of Mithala, one of India's

great householder sages whose name is synonymous with selfless action. When informed that his capital was on fire, he reportedly replied, "If Mithala is on fire, nothing of mine is on fire."

22 In verses 22, 23 and 24, the topic changes slightly and Krishna outlines the view that the cosmos has a gratuitous existence. That is, the world and all creatures existing in it are given existence gratis by the source of all that is. Nonetheless, we owe that source for giving us existence. Religious activity and spiritual endeavour result from our coming to grips with this reality. Hence, just as that source, personified in the poem as Krishna, freely gives in order that we may have existence, so should we freely give back by performing whatever duty the world manifests to us.

25 We now return to the argument that continues from verse 21. Humanity's actions are divided into wise and unwise. An argument is offered that all action results from how the gunas act on each other, that our ego causes us to think our actions are our own, that we should carry out our own duty without attachment, but that we shouldn't upset the minds of the unwise who do think they act.

30 With this verse and the next three the perspective shifts back to that of personalised Krishna that was introduced in verses 22 to 24. Intriguingly, after arguing about the need for the wise to have no sense of possession, Krishna now refers to this teaching of *mine* and decreeing that those carpers who reject *my* teaching are deluded and lost. From one perspective it could be said that the emotional tone behind these statements is at odds with the logical tone present in the verses that precede and follow verses 30, 31 and 32. On the other hand, it could be said the abstract teaching is given an emotional presentation for bhaktas who prefer a more personalised engagement with spiritual notions.

33 Here the text continues the line of thought from verse 29, which was interrupted by verses 30 to 32.

35 This verse has generated much discussion regarding if it en-

dorses caste distinctions. Philosophically, it serves to conclude the discussion of spiritualising action by performing one's duty, arguing that we each need to utilise the talents we are born with and apply them in whatever context we find ourselves. The idea some people have that they possess higher social or spiritual status due to their role, talents or situation has been shown to be erroneous in earlier verses that argue for even-mindedness and non-attachment.

36 What drives a man to do evil, against his own will, as if compelled by force? This question introduces part three of the discourse. Western metaphysics, shaped by Christian theology, has a problem with the existence of evil in the world, because God is defined as all-knowing, all-powerful and all-good. How, then, could a good God allow evil to exist and innocent people to be hurt? The text's view on the issue of evil is straightforward: we human beings create evil through our actions. Because it is we who do evil, it is in our power to eliminate evil from our lives.

42 The discourse ends with a reiteration of the chain of perception, knowledge and action. From lowest to highest, this chain is constituted of the senses, the mind, the intellect and atman. Because desires distract the senses, in order to establish an inner spiritual hierarchy in which action is carried out in a state of spiritual detachment, desire has to be eliminated from the chain. When that occurs desire no longer dominates the senses, the mind quietens, and the intellect is able to turn inward and focus on atman. The attributes of atman are then free to connect with the lower, material parts.

DISCOURSE FOUR

This discourse is titled, *The Yoga of Knowledge, Action and Sacrifice*. Structurally, the discourse has two parts. The first part ends at verse 15. It introduces the idea of Krishna being an avatar of Brahman, that is an incarnation, or embodied form, of the formless, transcendent, Absolute. Part two, which runs from verse 16, draws together the threads of thought offered in the previous two discourses by discussing the paths of knowledge and action—jnanayoga and karmayoga—in the context of sacrifice.

Sacrifice is central to Vedic rituals, particularly a ritual which involves burning clarified butter in a sacred fire. Ritual sacrifice, being performed physically, naturally takes place in the realm of action. The poet seeks to spiritualise sacrifice by lifting it out of the realm of ritual and into the sphere of spiritual endeavour. Verse 17 defines three kinds of action: action, illicit action and non-action. Non-action refers to action that is spiritualised when those acting do so while focused on atman within. Knowledge is seen as the key to spiritualising action, for only when the performer of an action is imbued with spiritual knowledge, derived from experience of atman, does that action not taint the performer. The discourse draws attention to the subtleties involved by examining sacrifice as a form of action.

However, before the second part's discussion of sacrifice begins, the discourse starts with fifteen verses that present Krishna as a personalised form of transcendent Brahman. The first verse has Krishna saying that he is now passing to Arjuna the same knowledge that he taught to sages who lived long ago.

1   Vivasat, Manu and Ikshvaka were royal sages who practised karmayoga at the dawn of Vedic civilisation. Little is known of them.

4   Arjuna's question elicits a response in which fascinating ideas regarding the cycles of birth, death and rebirth on both the cosmic and individual levels are presented.

5   *We have both had many births. I remember all mine; you know none.* Krishna's first level of response is that of an enlightened person who can remember his previous incarnations.

6   This verse lifts the discussion onto another level. Krishna asserts his identity with the unborn and undying purusha that manifested the cosmos via prakriti. Yogamaya refers to Brahman's power by which the material cosmos came into existence. Maya means veil, so the material manifest cosmos is seen as a veil that hides Krishna's unmanifest Being from

created beings. The metaphysical implication of the term yogamaya is that the material cosmos reveals the fact of the existence of Krishna's unmanifest Being, but at the same time hides the reality of what that Being actually is. Naturally, the man Krishna who is talking to Arjuna is not identical with this hidden unborn, transcendent, unmanifest Being. Thus when Krishna says that he is Lord of all beings, it needs to be interpreted in a metaphorical sense, not literally.

7 *Whenever right wanes and wrong prevails, know I am born in this world.* Krishna's birth as a manifestation of Brahman is now put into a human moral context. This approach reflects the concept of saviour gods which underpinned the Mediterranean mystery religions dating from the fifth century BCE, or earlier. The myths around Jesus Christ—that he was born of a virgin, that he was sacrificed and resurrected, that he ascended to heaven—are typical of stories told of the mystery gods. Such claims were also made for Krishna. In addition, the writer asserts that Krishna is a force for moral good, who is born to right wrongs and re-establish humanity's connection to Brahman.

8 Dharma is the path of righteousness, that is, teaching given to humanity for its spiritual realisation. In its lowest sense, dharma refers to an individual's religion; at its highest, the path by which seekers achieve spiritual realisation.

9 This verse asserts that, like the gods of the Mediterranean mystery religions, Krishna's birth and actions are mysterious. Verse 10 emphasises self-discipline and spiritual knowledge as providing the path towards mystical union with Krishna, and verse 11 distinguishes Krishna as the most catholic and non-sectarian of gods, saying worshippers do not have to worship Krishna personally, and that he will accept the worship of all, however they worship Brahman/God, and under whatever name.

15 *Ancient seekers acted in knowledge of this.* By referring to the ancients the writer brings the discussion back to the claim made by Krishna in verse 1 that he taught this yoga in ages

past. With the comments on Krishna completed, the discourse now moves on to discuss the nature of action.

17 Action consists of actions ordinarily carried out during the course of daily life; illicit action refers to action that is morally corrupt, harmful or spiritually contrary; non-action refers to the spiritual stillness at the heart of all action carried out in the material world.

18 This verse reinforces the idea that non-action exists at the core of all action, and that the way to transcend action and find wisdom is not through giving up action, but by entering the spiritual stillness that lies at the heart of all action.

19 The knowledge referred to here is spiritual knowledge derived from experience of atman. *Burns his actions* refers to sacrificing our actions by being non-attached while acting and not desiring whatever results from that action.

20 This verse defines the key to karmayoga: renouncing attachment to the results produced by action, and being even-minded during the performance of all action. Verses 21, 22 and 23 add to the definition of acting without being bound by karma through resting in non-action within action.

24 Having clarified how action may be spiritualised, the discourse now considers a special form of action—sacrifice. Ritual sacrifice is a core activity in all worship. Here the writer shifts the concept of sacrifice from an external ritual to it being an internalised spiritual process. The verse begins by asserting that everything existing is Brahman. Therefore, Brahman is not something to be worshipped as existing "out there", but is present in every action, including sacrifice.

25 Various types of sacrifice are now described, including those of hearing, of sense experience, of vital energy, of breath, of austerity, of diet or of learning. What these different forms of sacrifice share is that they require seekers to dedicate a fundamental aspect of their lives to achieve spiritual liberation. This variety of approaches also suggests that sacrifice is not a universal prescription, but varies according to each seeker's individual psychological make-up and inherent tal-

ents and abilities. Simply, we each have personal attributes to sacrifice. In this sense, sacrifice is not something we give up, but something we do. Thus the athlete gives up other activities and focuses on developing specific skills. Similarly, the seeker gives up certain activities in order to focus on developing spiritually. Then there is a higher level of sacrifice, in which the training and disciplines we carry out are offered up as sacrifice in the form of service.

31 To interpret this verse from a contemporary perspective, an action which has sacrifice at its core transforms the energy expended during that action into a higher form of energy. That energy then feeds and purifies the seeker's inward qualities and processes, resulting in self-transformation. The energy which purifies in this way is the higher energy that results from practising sacrifice.

32 *The Vedas describe many forms of sacrifice.* This phrase literally states that many forms of sacrifice are "set out in the mouth of Brahman". Because tradition maintains that the Vedas were spoken by Brahman, the text is usually translated as referring to the Vedas.

33 The idea the poem keeps returning to is that knowledge is the key to spiritualising action. Thus sacrifice necessarily has knowledge at its core. This knowledge is experiential knowledge of atman.

35 *You will see all beings in yourself, then in me.* What can be drawn from this assertion is that step one of spiritual realisation is seeing atman as existing within all beings, just as it exists within our own self. Thus, we adopt an even-minded attitude within and establish an identity with all beings. Step two is to see all beings, including ourselves, as unified in Brahman. We then see Brahman as all. This is Brahman-nirvana, the state in which all we perceive is experienced as unity, without separation or difference.

41 This verse reinforces the poem's teaching that simultaneously advocates the adoption of the inward qualities of self-discipline, purification and focus on atman, and the outward-

ly-directed attitude of remaining detached while performing actions. When the inwardly and outwardly directed aspects of action are held in balance, spiritual knowledge is achieved.

DISCOURSE FIVE

This discourse is titled *The Yoga of Sacrifice*. It extends the teaching on sacrifice offered in Discourse Four. The writer begins by having Arjuna ask a question: in order to obtain spiritual knowledge, should the seeker engage in action or withdraw from action?

This is a question that remains relevant today. In the past, spirituality has been conceived of as requiring seekers to give up a normal working life, leave one's family, and move to an ashram, monastery or zendo. In India many yogis have lived a totally secluded life of meditation. However, there is also a strong tradition of householder practice, in which seekers engage in spiritual disciplines while working and raising a family. The Taoists and Sufis also developed householder practices. Throughout the world today, the ashram or monastery is generally not seen as a long-term option, although many do use short retreats to clarify their purpose and help purify their inner processes. However, prayer and meditation, wherever and however briefly performed, also constitute periods of withdrawal and retreat. So Arjuna's question is about the need to find a balance between worldly action and withdrawal from worldly action.

Krishna's response to Arjuna's questions is not to answer the question directly—in fact, it has already been answered in the preceding discourse. Instead, the writer uses the question to further clarify the difference between karmayoga and sankhya (jnanayoga). Karmayoga involves engaging in the world and seeking the still spiritual centre of action. In contrast, jnanayoga involves withdrawing from the world and its activity, remaining inwardly focused while striving to maintain continuous experience of atman through meditation. To appreciate the difference between the paths of karmayoga and jnanayoga, it is useful to consider reality as consisting of manifest and unmanifest realms. Both are manifestations of Brahman. Karmayoga's practice comes out of an emphasis on the manifest realm, while jnanayoga's practice emphasises the unmanifest realm. Karmayoga uses a seeker's engagement with the world of action as its starting point, and then indicates a way of spiritualising that action so the seeker may eventually find the unmanifest spiritual realm which exists at the heart of the manifest realm. In contrast, jnanayoga focuses initially on the unmanifest realm, showing the seeker how to disengage from the manifest realm, renounce a life of active engagement with action, and exist in constant contact with the unmanifest while in a state of disengagement from the senses. This is achieved through meditation.

The discourse points out that karmayoga and jnanayoga have identical goals: the spiritual realisation that all existence is one in Brahman. However, the path taught by jnanayoga is difficult to sustain. As is observed in verse 6, continuous detachment from sense experience, through remaining seated in unmanifest atman, is difficult to achieve. Indeed, even the sankhya who practises jnanayoga needs to use karmayoga, because meditation is an action in which the seeker engages. As verse 20 points out, whatever we do, whether actively acting in the world or sitting in meditation, we should not be attached to or frustrated by the result; being *neither pleased with the pleasant nor disturbed by the unpleasant*. If we can rise above our own expectations, eventually, as verse 21 states, we will *find eternal bliss within*.

The discourse ends by returning to the goal of achieving of Brahman-nirvana, the state of experiencing Brahman the unified manifest and unmanifest realms. Throughout, the emphasis is on achieving spiritual knowledge in this life, while living in a body, rather than achieving knowledge after the body dies.

2   *Karmayoga is preferred to sanyasa*. The position maintained in this discourse is that while the practice of karmayoga and jnanayoga (also called sanyasa) equally enable the seeker to achieve spiritual realisation, karmayoga is more effective on a practical level. The remainder of this discourse explores the implications of this proposition.

7   This verse begins a sequence of comparisons between kar-

mayoga (practised by the yogi) and jnanayoga (performed by the sankhya). Another definition of the yogi who has mastered spiritualised action is offered here, which emphasises the inner qualities a yogi requires in order to act without being tainted by action. Verses 8 and 9 offer a description of the sankhya's experience. Essentially, the difference is that the yogi seeks stillness in the midst of movement, while the sankhya sits in the stillness while observing the movement of objects across the senses. These are two different ways of functioning, two different ways of being in the world.

11 A further difference is identified in that the yogi uses action itself as a means for achieving inner purification, through working on attitude, and restraining desires.

13 In contrast, the sankhya sits passively within the body, purifying the self through not touching or engaging with anything in the world. The body's nine gates are the ears, eyes, nostrils, mouth and the two organs of excretion.

18 A concluding section begins here, which describes the need to maintain an inner attitude of equanimity and evenmindedness, viewing all beings as equal.

25 For the karmayogi, realisation ends in the experience of Brahman-nirvana. But he or she still engages in action, using it to serve all beings.

26 Ascetic sankhyas, their awareness sunk deep in atman, experiences *Brahman-nirvana around them*. This experience leads to personal liberation. However, the knowledge they gain also enables them to serve, as India's great teachers have done.

In conclusion, the path of karmayoga offers a practice that enables the seeker to transform daily activity into a process for achieving purification. The aim is to make all work and activity a form of service. In contrast, the jnanayogi withdraws from everything and sustains a deep state of meditation in order to achieve freedom and knowledge, which is then made available to others.

DISCOURSE SIX

This discourse shifts the discussion to atman itself, offering a practice by which it may be experienced. Hence its title, *The Yoga of Steadfast, Concentrated Meditation on Atman*. The discourse has three parts: a general introduction from verse 1 to verse 9, a discussion of meditation practice between verses 10 and 36, and from verse 37 a discussion of what happens to those who adopt this practice but do not achieve spiritual realisation in this lifetime.

The first part begins by picking up a theme from the previous discourse, that of whether action or withdrawal is best. It begins by distinguishing between karmayoga and sanyasa. Sanyasa refers to renunciation, which is at the heart of jnanayoga, and therefore of the sankhya's practice. Karmayoga and sanyasa could be seen as opposed practices, insofar as the yogi engages in life while the sanyasa renounces it. Reflecting the previous discourse's conclusion, one of this discourse's purposes is to show that karmayoga and renunciation are two aspects of the one practice.

In verse 1, Krishna points out that both the sanyasi and the yogi equally have to do their duty without seeking rewards. While sanyasis have renounced the world, that does not mean they can decline to perform those actions required of them. On the other hand, verse 2 indicates that the yogi, like the sanyasi, is required to renounce worldly concerns, even while continuing to act in the world. Then, as verse 3 points out, action becomes a stepping stone towards eventual inner spiritual tranquillity. The virtue and necessity of practising equanimity, evenmindedness and self-discipline are then extolled once again.

Having concluded concepts arising from the previous discourse, the second part now begins, describing the practice of meditation. In verse 10 the writer suggests the seeker withdraw to the forest to meditate. Some scholars call those who wrote the earliest Upanishads forest philosophers, because they withdrew to live a solitary life in the forest in order to dedicate themselves to spiritual practices. This practice involves sitting still, focusing the mind, eschewing all thoughts, and learning to become immersed in atman. The goal is that once the meditator is able to centre on atman, Brahman-nirvana will eventually be experienced.

The discourse's third part starts in verse 33, with Arjuna objecting that the mind is restless, unstable and difficult to control, so he doesn't see how this meditation practice may be sustained. Krishna reassures him that it is indeed possible, through the practice of vairagya. *Vai* means to be dry or dried out, while *râga* means feeling and passion. Thus vairagya is the practice of dispassion, of being detached from worldly objects and activities. The writer points out it needs to be practised by both the karmayogi and the sanyasi. Each needs it in order to achieve the inner attitude of equanimity.

Arjuna then asks Krishna what becomes of those who strive on the yogic path, but fail to achieve the necessary self-discipline, or to attain to spiritual realisation. Krishna's response is that no effort is ever wasted, and that what is achieved in this life will be carried into the seeker's next incarnation.

This point raises two issues. One is that spiritual realisation is the result of many lives of effort, not just one. The difference in the level of achievement between seekers is therefore not one of potential—for all are capable of achieving the same realisation of Brahman-nirvana—it is rather that they have travelled a further or lesser distance along the path towards knowledge and liberation.

The second issue is the mechanism by which any person carries into this life the positive and negative qualities they have developed during their last incarnation, and so into their next. In Discourses Seven and Fifteen this process is discussed in greater detail. Here the idea is introduced.

10   The description offered here of *the disciplined yogi, living in seclusion, alone, devoid of desires and possessions*, contradicts Krishna's call for Arjuna to go out onto the battlefield, do his duty as a warrior, use the weapons he possesses, and kill his kin. On the other hand, the practice of sitting calmly and learning to centre within enables the warrior to sustain dispassion in the midst of battle.

14   Brahmacharya is a practice in which the seeker observes the

cardinal and casual vows Vedanta teaches by which Brahman may be attained. The cardinal vows are non-violence, truthfulness, non-stealing, celibacy and non-possession. The casual vows are bodily purity, contentment, the study of the scriptures, austerity and meditation on Brahman.

20 In this and the following verses, atman with a lower case "a" refers to the individual spiritual self, whereas Atman with an upper case "A" refers to purusha, the spiritual vibration which transcends the individual self.

28 *The purified yogi, merged with Atman, then feels the endless bliss of bonding with Brahman.* Here Brahman and Atman (purusha) are seen as identical, being just different perspectives for considering, the experience of spiritual unity. In verse 30, perception of Krishna is also declared to be identical with the experience of Brahman and Atman. Thus the worship of a personalised form of God leads to an experience of the transcendent Absolute, which has many names and is described in multiple ways, but however named is the one state.

DISCOURSE SEVEN

Having spent six discourses describing the nature of spiritual experience, and proposing yogic practices that lead the seeker to that experience, the discussion now widens to consider the nature of the cosmos and our existence in it, as indicated by the title, *The Yoga of Knowledge of the Manifest and the Unmanifest.*

The manifest is the physical world; the unmanifest is the subtle spiritual realm experienced via atman. An explication of the nature of the manifest physical and unmanifest spiritual realms, and their relationship, begins in this discourse and continues through to Discourse Fifteen. Topics include how the cosmos came into existence, how prakriti and purusha function in the cosmos, how body and atman are connected to produce human experience, and how, as spiritual beings, we move between the manifest and unmanifest realms via the cycle of birth, death and rebirth.

2   In this verse, the poet uses the terms jnana and vijnana. In English, jnana is translated as knowledge, while vijnana is usually translated as discriminatory knowledge, or, more simply, discrimination. The question then arises: discrimination with respect to what? The way vijnana is translated depends on our answer to this question. Among the *Bhagavad Gita's* many commentators, Shankara interprets jnana and vijnana as knowledge and experience, Tilak suggests vijnana refers to knowledge of the physical world, and Desai considers jnana to refer to the experience of the self, and vijnana to knowledge of the self as existing separate from that which is not-self. Clearly, any translation of the linked terms jnana and vijnana needs to arise out of a considered reading of the poem itself.

In terms of humanity's experience of reality, a distinction is maintained throughout the *Gita* between the physical realm we experience via our senses and the spiritual realm we experience via atman. Paired concepts such as prakriti (matter) and purusha (spirit), prakriti (the material realm) and jiva (the spiritual being), body and atman, and higher and lower, are maintained throughout. In the light of this dual concept of reality, the translation offered in this verse, and in what follows, is that jnana refers to knowledge of the manifest realm, and vijnana to knowledge of the unmanifest realm.

4   *Earth, water, fire, air, ether, mind, intellect, ego—eightfold is my prakriti divided.* These eight are presented as the key categories of humanity's psychophysical existence. They are drawn from Sankhya philosophy.

5   Jiva is the spiritual essence (atman) of a living entity.

8   The *Upanishads* argue that Brahman underpins all the innumerable forces that function in the world. In earlier times, which were dominated by mythological ways of thinking, these forces were called gods. Here Krishna, like Brahman, is identified as the single source of all the various gods. In effect, everything is Krishna's manifestation.

14 Maya means illusion. The view of all Indian philosophies is

that the physical cosmos is illusory, in the sense that it is impermanent, and that it is dependent for its existence on Brahman. There is much debate regarding how illusory the world is. Shankara argued the physical realm is entirely illusory, with no real existence. Ramanuja argued it has a contingent but real existence—that is, the cosmos depends on the Absolute for its existence, which continues to exist while all else comes and goes, but that if we get hit by a bus, while it is both a contingent and a real bus. Whatever the subtleties of their interpretations, Indian philosophers agree that real and true knowledge consists of knowledge of Brahman, the Absolute. Krishna again equates himself with Brahman.

15 This verse introduces the idea that there are two fundamental natures: the demonic and the divine. Previously, there have been references to people being ignorant, being stained by their actions, and therefore sinful, and as having fallen from the way, but not of being demonic. Here, the attitude towards people who have not found the spiritual path is more condemning. This attitude is contrary to the even-mindedness and equanimity advocated in earlier discourses. Discourse Sixteen expounds on this differentiation between the so-called divine and demonic natures in much greater detail.

19 Vasudeva is a compound word, consisting of *vásu*, good, and *deva*, deity. By the second century BCE, a monotheistic Indian sect worshipped a single, supreme God under the name of Vasudeva. However, there was another Vasudeva, in Indian mythology the father of Krishna. Over time, Krishna came to be called not just the son of Vasudeva, but Vasudeva himself. In the *Bhagavad Gita*, Krishna is identified with Vasudeva as the single, supreme Being.

21 An argument begins here that due to the principle of reciprocity we obtain what we worship. Thus if we worship a particular form of God, we achieve a connection with that form. In psychospiritual terms, we create our own religious reality through our own thinking and desiring. Hence some Christian saints sought a vision of Jesus or Mary, while oth-

ers wanted to have Christ's stigmata on their body. Similarly, Indian worshippers cry out for visions of Kali, Vishnu or Ram. The author says here that the formless Power that underlies and transcends reality ensures each worshipper receives what they desire. But the idea that underpins the *Bhagavad Gita*, and that is offered again in verse 23, is that these are all limited perspectives. True knowledge and deep perception result when we transcend all forms of the Absolute, those forms being our creation.

23 Vedic religion taught that the goal of worship was to go to the heaven of the gods, and that it was reached after the body's death as a result of accruing moral merit. Further comments on this idea are made in Discourse Nine, verses 20 and 21.
24 The argument is closed with the assertion that to think the Supreme has a definite form is ignorance, while in verse 25 Krishna states that his yogamaya—the manifest cosmos—hides his Reality from view.
29 The discourse ends by identifying six key terms: Brahman, adhyatma, karma, adhibhuta, adhidaiva and Adhiyajna. An explanation of what they are is provided at the beginning of the next discourse.

DISCOURSE EIGHT

This discourse continues the discussion begun in the preceding discourse. It starts by defining the six terms introduced at the end of Discourse Seven. Why these six? Presumably, the terms were being intensely debated at the time of writing, and a definitive meaning was offered to close down what may have been endless intellectual speculation and argument. Only the term Brahman is discussed elsewhere.

Having discussed these six, the discourse then moves on to its main purpose: to describe the process by which the yogi escapes rebirth, to explain the processes by which human beings are reborn, and to introduce a vision of how the cosmos itself was born, dies, and is reborn again. This vision is one of the great metaphysical contributions made by the writers of the *Bhagavad Gita*, and has drawn attention due to the way its vision resonates with the theory of the Big Bang.

The process of dying and not being reborn is discussed from verse 5 to verse 15. The author suggests various strategies: focusing on Krishna at the moment of death (verse 5), being disciplined in meditation at all times (verses 8, 9 and 10), and closing the nine gates of the body, fixing the life-breath in the forehead, and repeating Om (verses 12 and 13). The point is made in verse 6 that at the moment of death whatever our mind is absorbed in, whatever our thoughts are clinging to, we go to. This also dictates the conditions of rebirth. An illustration of this was provided by events that occurred in India when I was living in Shri Muniji's ashram in Rajasthan, working on this version. During this period Rajiv Gandhi was assassinated by a bomb attack while campaigning for election. Shri Muniji commented that because Rajiv Gandhi's thoughts were focused on politics at the moment he died, he would be reborn into a political context.

Verse 10 points out that by dying in a state of meditation, with the breath fixed between the brows, the yogi will achieve freedom. However, this is a long way from the Kshatriyas, the warriors whose duty is to go out and die in battle. The emphasis here is on dying in a state of seated meditation, with no significant comment made regarding the best way to die while engaged in action. Presumably this discourse was produced by a writer who was not a warrior, but for whom sitting meditation was a principal form of practice. Of relevance here is Discourse Four, verse 17 and following, which discusses the practice of non-action within actio, and so indicates how a warrior may be in a dispassionate state while dying in battle.

From verse 16 the discussion offers metaphysical speculation regarding how the cosmos itself is born, dies and is reborn. This cycle is seen as on-going, with all beings manifested by purusha eventually being absorbed back into purusha, and being manifested again. In verses 18 and 19, the process is likened to Brahma's day and night, Brahma being the creator God of Vedic mythology. However, the underlying conceptual framework remains that of Sankhya philosophy, with purusha being named the ultimate unmanifest from which all the cosmos emanates, and into which, at the end of its cycle, the cosmos is re-absorbed.

This idea excited much interest from physicists in the early twentieth century, because it accorded with one of the implications of Einstein's theory of relativity. At the time Einstein offered his theory it was widely thought that the cosmos existed in a steady state—that it had always existed, and would always exist. But as scientists began to explore the implications of Einstein's theory, it was seen to offer a vision of the cosmos coming into existence via an explosion that manifested via a singularity, an event now known as the big bang. The theory also offered three possible cosmic outcomes: the cosmos could keep expanding forever, it could expand to a certain point and remain there at equilibrium, or it could expand to a certain point, then contract again until, in the big crunch, it vanished back into a singularity. The third possibility clearly accords with the vision of the cosmic cycle offered in this discourse.

This discourse is titled *The Yoga of Brahman*. It begins by naming Brahman's principal manifestations, then reconciles the concept of Brahman with the ideas that underpin Sankhya philosophy. In addition, it includes a half-dozen references to Krishna. If, while reading, the reader replaces these references to Krishna with the name of Brahman, it will be seen that the whole discourse reads perfectly well as a description of Brahman, its manifest attributes, and the way experiential knowledge of Brahman may be achieved.

3   The name Brahman is derived from the Sanskrit root word *brhm*, which means to expand, to grow. Adhyatma is Brahman's manifestation in individual spiritual selves. For comments on karma, see the preceeding essay on the *Bhagavad Gita's* philosophy.

4   Adhibhuta is the sum of all forms. It could be thought of as referring to all the manifest cosmos being Brahman's body. Adhidaiva is the individual purusha, otherwise known as at-

man, which exists within those forms. Adhiyajna literally means "the greatest sacrifice". By referring to himself as Adhiyajna, Krishna is stating that Brahman makes a sacrifice when it incarnates within a body as an individual spiritual self. This provides another aspect of the teaching, given in Discourse Five, that it is by sacrifice that the seeker achieves knowledge of Brahman. In accordance with the principle of reciprocity, the Absolute made a sacrifice in order to emanate the cosmos, while beings in that cosmos are required to make a sacrifice in order to know that from which they emanate.

11   For brahmacharya, see the note on Discourse Six, verse 14.

16   Brahmaloka is a term from Vedic mythology. It refers to the heavenly realm of the creator god, Brahma. This realm forms the upper limit of the material universe. Brahma, the creator god, should not be confused with Brahman, the Absolute.

17   According to Vedic mythology Brahma's day is the period of the cosmos' manifestation, a thousand yugas is 4,320,000,000 years, and Brahma's night is the period when the cosmos is re-absorbed by Brahma.

18   Brahmaloka is identified with unmanifest prakriti, thus reconciling Vedic mythology and Sankhya philosophy. An interesting metaphysical question rises here: is the manifest cosmos re-absorbed into unmanifest prakriti, i.e. into a state of energetic material potential, or is everything, including prakriti, re-absorbed into purusha? Verse 20 answers this.

20   This verse suggests that, at the end of each cosmic cycle, only purusha exists. Prakriti is unmanifest matter and energy, but it is the contingent unmanifest. Here it is stated that purusha is the ultimate Unmanifest, which solely exists at the beginning and end of each cosmic cycle. Note, however, that verse 7 in the following discourse offers an alternative view.

23   This and the next four verses are contentious. Presumably, these verses refer to a religious belief regarding rebirth, the full details of which are now lost. This belief suggests that the time of year people die dictates whether they are reborn or escape rebirth. Clearly, this contradicts the earlier verses

which state that the key to escaping rebirth is being focused on the Unmanifest at the moment of death.

24 *Fire, light, the bright fortnight, the sun's six-month northern course.* This idea, also referred to in the *Rig Veda* and the *Upanishads* (see *Chûndogya Upanishad* 5.10 1-6), suggests that in Vedic times a belief was held that it was more propitious to die in certain times of the year than others. (It was because of this belief that the warrior Bhishma, mentioned in the opening discourse, waited before allowing himself to die.) It is not known where such a belief came from. Tilak suggests the Aryan peoples may have originated from the polar regions, and that references to the sun's sixth month northern and southern courses reflect a folk memory of the long arctic days and nights. However, no archaeological evidence supports this explanation, and it is not widely accepted.

25 Another ancient belief was that the heavenly realm existed beneath the lunar sphere, and that those who attained only to the lunar realm were reborn. Those who reached the solar sphere above it attained to Brahman and were not reborn.

26 *Bright and dark—these two are deemed the eternal paths of the world.* The author offers a metaphorical interpretation of these ancient beliefs, suggesting the paired descriptors represent in a general sense humanity's spiritual choice of following the path of knowledge and escaping rebirth, or following the path of ignorance and being reborn.

DISCOURSE NINE

Discourses Nine, Ten, Eleven and Twelve focus on Krishna as a manifestation of Brahman, and on the worship of Krishna in both his unmanifest reality and his manifest form. The sequence of discourses starts with this, titled *The Yoga of the King of Sciences and the King of Secrets*. The science and secret referred to is worship of Krishna. However, the Krishna to be worshipped is not a personal god, but the Supreme Being, the creator, sustainer and destroyer of all that is. As verses 4 and 5 state, this Supreme Being pervades the cosmos and contains all beings, but is neither contained in nor bound by any being.

Much in this discourse reiterates what has been stated earlier, particularly points made in Discourse Seven. The view of Vasudeva as the object of worship is repeated and expanded here. The point is made in verse 7 that the process by which Krishna, as unmanifest Being, emanates and re-absorbs the cosmos, is via prakriti. This could be read as a response to what is proposed in verse 20 of the preceding discourse, that says the cosmos emanates from and is reabsorbed into purusha; this discourse states that everything in the manifest cosmos emanates from, and returns to, prakriti, a process which Krishna, as supreme Being, initiates: *When a kalpa ends, all beings merge with my prakriti; when the next begins, I project them out again.* This question as to whether the cosmos resolves back into prakriti or purusha is taken up again in verse 3 of Discourse Fourteen.

7   A kalpa is the period of Brahma's cosmic day, i.e. the period the cosmos exists between its manifestation and reabsorption.

12   This and verse 13 repeat the idea of people having divine or demonic natures, first introduced in verse 15 of Discourse Seven. See the note on that verse, and Discourse Sixteen.

17   Om is the sacred syllable signifying Brahman, the Absolute. The *Rig, Saman* and *Yujas* are the three principal books of the Vedas.

20   The drinking of the juice of soma refers to an ancient religious ritual of which no details are known today. Some scholars suggest it had a narcotic or psychedelic effect that induced trance and mystical states.

21   *That vast realm enjoyed, and all merit spent, they then return to the world of mortals.* This refers to an early concept of karmic results in which it was contended that religious worshippers who built up karmic merit went to heaven after their body's death. They remained in heaven, enjoying themselves for as long as their karmic merit lasted. When their merit was depleted, they were reborn into another body.

23 This verse echoes Discourse Seven, verse 21.
24 This expands on Discourse Seven, verse 23.
32 This verse made Shri Muniji uncomfortable. He wanted the references to caste removed, as he considered casteism to be a blight on India, and the reference to it here to be unworthy of the *Bhagavad Gita's* high aspirations. The verse has been translated in accordance with the traditionally accepted meaning so the reader may make up his or her own mind regarding the attitudes that underpin it.

DISCOURSE TEN

This discourse and the next offer a vision of Krishna as the Supreme Being who emanates, sustains and absorbs the cosmos. Gods and characters drawn from Indian mythology are used to portray Krishna's vast powers.

The discourse begins by describing Krishna as the transcendent source of all, and how all the virtues and attributes that enable seekers to approach Krishna—fortitude, truthfulness, serenity, equanimity, generosity, and so on—come from Krishna himself. The majority of the discourse is devoted to Krishna answer to Arjuna's question in verse 17, in which he describes his own power and its manifestations. Accordingly, the discourse is titled, *The Yoga of Supernal Qualities*. These qualities are given largely in terms of Vedic mythology, extending the descriptions of Krishna's power and manifestations offered in Discourse Seven, verses 8-11, and Discourse Nine, verses 16-19.

6 The seven great seers are Mariachi, Angiras, Atri, Pulstya, Pulaha, Kratu and Vasishtha. Very little is known of any of them, including who they were and when they lived. The ancient four is an unknown reference. The Manus are traditionally numbered fourteen. Each is supposed to reign in turn for the period of a kalpa (a period of 4,320 million years).
13 Narada, Asita, Devala and Vyasa were ancient seers. The last is traditionally regarded as the author of the *Bhagavad Gita*.
14 Kesheva is an epithet for Krishna. It denotes Krishna as the

triune deity who combines in himself the creator Brahma, the sustainer Vishnu, and the destroyer Shiva.

21 The Adityas are a group of gods. In some texts, the Adityas number twelve and are associated with the twelve months; in others, they number, seven or eight. Vishnu is widely worshipped as the greatest of all the Indian gods. The Maruts were the forty-nine wind gods.

22 Because it contains the best devotional chants, the *Sama Veda* is held to be the foremost *Veda*. Indra is the king of the heavenly powers.

23 The Rudras are the eleven gods of destruction. Kubera is the lord of wealth. His treasures were guarded by the Yaksas and Rakshashas. The Vasus are personifications of fire, wind, dawn, etc. Meru is the mountain around which the planets are traditionally supposed to revolve. It is purported to be full of gems and riches.

24 Bhihaspati is the teacher of Indra, king of the heavenly powers. Skanda, also known as Kartikeya, is the god of war, equivalent to the Roman god, Mars.

25 Bhrigu was a great seer in ancient times. Japa is the repetition of one of God's names.

26 Ashvattha is the sacred peepul tree. See Discourse Fourteen for a fuller description. Narada was an ancient sage and musician, whose songs worshipped Krishna as an avatar of Vishnu. Chitrarathra led the Ghandharvas, celestial musicians and actors. Kapila is considered to be the originator of Sankhya philosophy.

27 According to Vedic mythology, the gods once churned the ocean in order to obtain nectar. As a result of this churning, the ocean yielded fourteen objects. Airavata, which became Indra's elephant, is one of these objects. Uchchaihshravas is another of the fourteen objects. He became Indra's horse.

28 Vajra is Indra's thunderbolt, made of the bones of the sage Dadhichi, who immolated himself to save the world. Kamadhenu is another of the fourteen objects. It is a divine cow that can fulfil all desires. Kandarpa, later commonly known

as Kâmadeva, is the god of love. Vasuki is the king of the serpents. The gods used him as a rope with which to churn the ocean to produce nectar.
29 Ananda is the thousand-hooded snake on which Indra sits. Varuna, in pre-Vedic times, was a thunder god, equivalent to Thor and Zeus. Later he became lord of the waters. Aryaman is the sun god. Yama is ruler of the dead.
30 Prahlada was an ideal devotee who braved his father's wrath and endured many trials rather than give up his devotion to God. Garuda is the bird ridden by Indra.
31 The reference to Rama is unclear. He could be the warrior Parashurama, or the Rama of the *Ramayama*.
35 Brihat Saman is a hymn in the *Sama Veda*, in the brihati metre. Gayatr is a metre that contains the quintessence of all hymns. In ancient times, Margashirsha was the first month of the year.
37 Vasudeva: see note on Discourse 7, verse 17. Vyasa is revered as the compiler of the *Vedas*. The reference to Ushanas is unclear. He could be god of the serpents, or an ancient sage or poet.

DISCOURSE ELEVEN

This discourse presents one of the greatest visions of God in all world literature. It follows on from the previous discourse, which ends with Krishna stating that *with but a part of myself, I support this whole cosmos as I stand*. At the start of this discourse, Arjuna asks to see Krishna in his cosmic form, as Ishvara, the personalised aspect of transcendent, formless Brahman, who supports the cosmos. Krishna grants Arjuna's request, temporarily giving him divine vision so he may see Krishna in all his cosmic glory. Thus the discourse's title, *The Yoga of the Vision of the Cosmic Form*. Philosophically, this can only be an illusion, because Brahman is formless and transcends all perception. However, human beings find it difficult to worship an abstraction. Therefore this vision helps worshippers envisage the extent of Krishna's power, and have an image, however limited it must be in reality, of transcendent Brahman.

What is interesting is the form in which it is offered. This is not the Krishna of popular Indian religion, the cow herder who plays the flute and dances in the field with beautiful gopis (milk maids). Rather, this vision offers a Krishna who is not safe or comforting at all—to the extent that Arjuna is terrified by what he sees. Initially, in verses 5 to 22, this terror is from the sheer power and scope of Krishna, with sages, divine beings and gods all existing as a tiny part of his cosmic body. But as verse 10 notes, Krishna also holds *countless uplifted weapons of death*. Thus, from verse 23, this vision becomes one of Krishna as destroyer. The vision ties into the poem's overall theme by having Arjuna see all the warriors who are about to engage in battle as already dead, crushed by Krishna's teeth, being lapped up by his numerous tongues, and falling into his multiple flaming mouths. From verse 32, Krishna returns to Arjuna's statement that he will not fight, which has initiated Krishna's entire exposition, and offers yet another reason why Arjuna should take part in the battle. Arjuna's response is to bow down and worship Krishna as an embodiment of the transcendent spiritual reality. Krishna concludes by saying that no one can see his radiant, primal, infinite cosmic form through studying the *Vedas*, offering gifts, engaging in ritualistic worship, or by carrying out austerities. Rather, this vision is only offered by Krishna to his devotees, as a result of their devotion.

3   Ishvara is God as a personalised aspect of Brahman, in this case, Krishna himself.

6   The Adityas are a group of gods mentioned in various texts. In places, the Adityas number twelve and are associated with the twelve months; in others, they number, seven or eight. The Vasus are eight nature gods, representing fire, wind, sky, etc. The Rudras are the gods of destruction. The twin Ashwins had various functions. They were divine horsemen, symbolised dawn and dusk, and served as physicians to the gods. The Maruts are storm gods.

15   Rishis are great seers. Tradition maintains a group of enlight-

ened rishis lived in the dawn of Vedic civilisation. Brahma is the creator god in Indian mythology.

18 Dharma is the path of righteousness, which leads to truth and knowledge.

21 Siddhas possess various powers, some spiritual, some psychic. Maharishis are great seers. The traditional difference between siddhas and rishis is that rishis see into reality, whereas siddhas both see into reality and have the power to enable others to see.

22 Sadhyas are another group of celestial beings. Their exact nature and function is unclear. Manes are the ancestral spirits. Gandharvas are celestial musicians, often part horse or bird, who act as messengers between humanity and the gods. Yaksas are nature spirits. In early Vedic mythology, Asuras appear to have represented moral qualities. In later times, they were associated with demonic qualities, and opposed to the Devas (gods).

37 Mahatman is a great soul or being.

39 Vayu is the wind god. Yama is ruler of the dead, and particularly of purgatory, where people go to be purged of their sins. Agni is an ancient god of fire, who remains current in Indian worship because of his association with the fire of religious worship. Varuna is an ancient storm god, associated with the sky and thunder. Shashanka is the moon. Prajapati is an ancient name for the creator god. He was later associated with Brahma. The Ancient is Brahma's grandfather.

42 Krishna was born into the Yadava tribe, becoming their king.

DISCOURSE TWELVE

Having just presented an intoxicating—if terrifying—vision of Krishna as a personification of the unmanifest Absolute, Discourse Twelve begins with Arjuna asking whether it is better for seekers to worship Brahman in a personalised form, or to eschew all forms and immerse themselves in the unmanifest. Seekers worship Krishna as Brahman via the manifest world when they engage in karmayoga and bhaktiyoga, when they strive to worship and surrender all they are to Krishna. Seekers worship Krishna as Brahman via the unmanifest realm when they withdraw from all worldly activities, make the senses passive, and, through the practice of silent meditation, strive to remain immersed in atman for extensive periods. Which is the best path?

Krishna replies that both equally lead to experiential knowledge of Brahman. However, he states in verse 5 that *it is difficult for those whose minds are fixed always on the unmanifest, for it is challenging to sustain oneness with the unmanifest while in the body.* That is, it is easier to practice karmayoga and bhaktiyoga, while living an ordinary daily existence, dedicating actions to God, and always striving to remember God.

Verses 8 to 12 answer the question in more detail by offering a hierarchy of practice. Verse 8 emphasises the importance of meditation, whereby mind and intellect are immersed in atman and focused on Brahman. Verse 9 says that if we are unable to sustain this, then we should maintain the constant practice of yoga, although it is unclear exactly what form of yoga is being referred to. Verse 10 says that if we are unable to constantly practise yoga, we should concentrate on serving God. Verse 11 says that if we are unable to sustain service, we should subdue our desires, dedicate all we do to God, and surrender the results of our work to God.

As a hierarchy, this is somewhat hazy, due to the lack of clarity as to precisely what is intended in each stage. However, it is clear that meditation is the highest form of practice, and abandoning the fruit of action the lowest. But verse 12 overturns this by suggesting that renouncing action's fruit is a higher practice than meditation. Arguably, hierarchy doesn't matter. Because there are different paths towards Brahman, providing different ways of attaining spiritual knowledge. The pragmatic resolution of this quandary is that whatever practices work for us, those are the practices we should take up.

The remainder of the discourse, from verse 13, outlines the characteristics of the perfect seeker. These characteristics are a reiteration of what has been stated earlier. Collectively, they describe *The Yoga of Devotion*.

DISCOURSE THIRTEEN

Discourses Nine to Twelve explore the relationship of the manifest to unmanifest realm by evoking a powerful image of Krishna as a form of Brahman, and describing the qualities a seeker needs in order to worship such a form. Discourses Thirteen, Fourteen and Fifteen take a different tack, offering an analysis of the way that we humans, who combine a physical body and a spiritual atman, participate in the manifest and unmanifest realms.

Discourse Thirteen begins by defining the basis of human experience. The concepts and technical terms used are again drawn from the *Upanishads* and Sankhya philosophy, leading to a repetition of earlier ideas. But what is interesting here is that this discourse offers a phenomenological analysis of the way our consciousness is constructed, and the process by which we experience the manifest and unmanifest domains.

This analysis naturally leads to a consideration of the nature of knowledge, because our knowledge necessarily derives from our experience: if we didn't experience anything, we could never have knowledge of anything. Conversely, we also use our knowledge to interpret what we experience. So what we know and what we experience are linked: together, they shape our awareness.

One of the *Bhagavad Gita's* core ideas is that the aim of human striving is to achieve experiential spiritual knowledge. Knowledge teaches us what we need to do in order to achieve spiritual understanding; knowledge provides us with a practical path of spiritual endeavour; and knowledge is also the goal we wish to achieve. In all these forms knowledge is not something we gain through book learning: we gain knowledge via direct experience.

The writer begins by dividing our experience into three aspects. First is the body, which is called the field. Second is our personal awareness as the experiencer of the body, called the knower of the field. Third is knowledge, which consists of knowledge of the field and of the knower of the field. All three exist within Brahman, which verse 2 describes as the *knower of the field in all fields*.

The field, knowledge and what is known are outlined in verses 5 to 17. Verses 5 and 6 define the field of experience. This field is not limited to the human body, but incorporates all material reality and what enables us to experience that reality. That reality includes unmanifest prakriti, the organs and senses by which our bodies experience the world, and the objects of action and sense experience. Verses 7 to 11 define knowledge as those virtues which seekers need to practise in order to detach themselves from the manifest physical realm so they can experience the unmanifest spiritual realm. Verses 12 to 17 define what is ultimately to be known: unmanifest Brahman, which transcends the material cosmos, yet is present in it.

The analysis now extends to identifying the field and the knower of the field in terms of Sankhya philosophy. The field is identified with prakriti and with the modulations of the gunas, while the knower of the field is identified with purusha (atman) which experiences the field. Knowledge is defined as consisting of knowledge of prakriti, the gunas and purusha. Through gaining knowledge of these aspects of Brahman, the seeker will not be reborn. All knowledge is achieved as a result of personal effort. In verses 24 and 25, various paths are identified as equally valid for gaining experiential knowledge. Meditation, jnanyoga, karmayoga and bhaktiyoga are specifically identified.

The discourse ends with a reminder that the manifest realm derives from, and is filled by, Brahman, and that ultimately spiritual knowledge derives from our direct perception of this reality. Further, we come to this knowledge through experiencing atman, our spiritual self. Thus, as far as our individual experience is concerned, atman illuminates the field of our experience. And it is through atman that we transcend the manifest material realm of prakriti, escape rebirth, and achieve oneness with Brahman.

4   The *Brahma Sutras* are one of the three basic texts of Vedanta. The other two are the *Upanishads* and the *Bhagavad Gita*.

5   The five elements are earth, air, fire, water and ether. The ten organs are the five senses plus the five organs of action: the hands, the feet, the tongue and the two organs of excretion.
6   By cohesion is meant the state by which all the various aspects of the body, including its organs, senses and awareness, function collectively to provide us with subjective experience.
13 This verse reminds us of the vision of Krishna in the preceding discourse, but places that vision within a philosophic context. What are Brahman's feet that walk, hands that clasp, ears that hear, eyes that see? Obviously, Brahman transcends the manifest realm, so has no feet, eyes, and so forth. Yet, because Brahman exists everywhere, it is through creatures that Brahman walks, clasps, hears and sees.

DISCOURSE FOURTEEN

This discourse continues the discussion offered in the previous discourse, extending the analysis of the three gunas and placing them into a psychological context. In the context of what we know today of the human psychological make-up, this analysis is understandably lacking a great deal. However, seen in the historical context of European psychology, which was initially grounded in Aristolean virtues and Christianity's seven deadly sins, with negative traits being identified during the Middle Ages with animal charcateristics (sly as a fox, innocent as a dove, etc.), the *Bhagavad Gita's* approach, while somewhat abstract, has the advantage of focusing character traits back onto the individual's behaviour.

The three qualities of the gunas are sattva, rajas and tamas. While they exist in a hierarchy, ultimately all three have to be transcended in order to achieve freedom. Thus, as verse 14 observes, even good people, imbued with sattvic qualities such as generosity and luminosity, are reborn. Only those who transcend the gunas altogether, through experiencing atman, achieve knowledge and freedom from rebirth.

The final section, from verse 21, defines the qualities the illuminated seeker needs to acquire.

DISCOURSE FIFTEEN

Titled *The Yoga of Purushotthama*—Purushotthama means Supreme Being—this discourse again examines the relationship between the manifest and unmanifest aspects of reality. It also offers further thoughts on the process of rebirth.

The discourse begins by using the metaphor of the tree of life to explicate the spiritual task. In India, the tree of life is associated with the fig, the ashvattha. Two varieties of fig were considered especially sacred, the banyan and the peepal, because their roots grew up as well as down, thus symbolising the complexity of life. The point is made here that we must cut through the entanglements of life by wielding the axe of detachment.

Verses 7 to 10 then add another statement regarding the process by which reincarnation occurs. These verses describe how the individual jiva (embodied atman) draws around itself the senses and mind, each aspects of prakriti. Discourse Eight has asserted that whatever we are thinking of at the moment of death is what we go to after death. If the self is sufficiently purified, we go to Brahman, but if we attached to the body and material existence, we are reborn. Applying that principle to the statement made in this discourse, we can see that the level of purification of the senses and mind that "clothe" atman dictate where atman goes after its current body dies. Verse 8 states, *As the wind carries scents from flower-beds, so the Lord of the body takes these six when it discards one body and travels on to another birth*. Thus the qualities we develop in one life, positive or negative, cling to us after our body dies, and we carry them into our next life.

Discourse Thirteen, verse 21, further states, *Purusha, seated in prakriti, experiences the gunas produced by prakriti; attachment to the gunas then causes purusha's birth in good or evil homes*. Thus the argument is developed that the gunic qualities in which we engage through the choices and efforts we make contribute to our individual being vibration. Discourse Fourteen, verse 18, states, *Those abiding in sattva rise upwards; those in rajas remain in the middle; while those in tamas sink into the depths*. This suggests that we carry whichever gunic qualities predominate in us during this lifetime into our next body. The gunic qualities apply not just to moral and psychological attitudes, but also the talents we develop, the useful and destructive habits we cultivate, and our emotional qualities and intellectual abilities. Therefore there are two sets of factors that dictate the qualities we possess in our next birth: the attachments of the senses and mind, and the moral, psychological, artistic, physical, emotional and intellectual talents and qualities that we have cultivated during this and previous lives.

The discourse ends with an assertion that supreme Being transcends both the perishable and imperishable. The perishable is the material world, the imperishable is unmanifest prakriti. However, beyond both these is Paramatman (Supreme Self or Supreme Soul), also named Ishvara, the personalised aspect of transcendent, formless Brahman. Both these offer different ways to conceptualise Purushotthama, supreme Being.

1 Ashvattha is the peepul (fig) tree, the name of which means "that which will not last even until tomorrow". It is depicted here as upside down, indicating the upside down nature of human experience, due to sensory inpts dominating everyday human experience.

7 Jiva literally means creature. The human jiva is defined here as consisting of atman plus the attributes of the senses and mind. These six attributes enable atman to experience the world. If they are full of attachments, they lead to atman's rebirth in another body.

14 The vaishvanara fire maintains the body's temperature. The four varieties of food are eaten, sucked, licked and drunk.

DISCOURSE SIXTEEN

Discourse Sixteen focuses on the difference between those who are born with divine qualities and those born with demonic qualities. This distinction between divine and demonic is first made in Discourse Seven, verse 9, and subsequently in Discourse Nine, verses 12 and 13. However, in Discourse Seven the demonic is characterised as a way of living that people embrace, whereas in Discourse Nine people are described as having a demonic nature. In this discourse, verse 4 states that people are born with a demonic nature. There is are substantial variations in the use of the concept of demonic in these three discourses. Discourse Three suggests that people enter a demonic way of living, the implication being that they choose to do so, while Discourse Nine proposes that some people are born with a demonic nature. Is acting evilly primarily a matter of choice and therefore of behaviour—as stated in Discourses Three and Seven—or a matter of birth, and a part of innate psychospiritual nature, as stated in Discourses Nine and Sixteen? Three issues are worth considering in relation to this question.

First, this discourse's analysis of people being either divine or demonic differs from the psychospiritual teaching of the gunas, which categorises people as being either sattvic, rajasa or tamasa. Verse 4 here identifies demonic qualities as including hypocrisy, arrogance, self-importance, anger, incivility and ignorance. These are psychological traits manifested by those who are rajasa and tamasa. Is the division into divine and demonic more illuminating than identifying human qualities as either sattvic, rajasa or tamasa?

Second, this discourse projects a degree of judgement that contradicts the principle of equanimity that is proposed in earlier discourses, where those who ignore the teaching are defined as ignorant or deluded rather than demonic. In particular, verse 19 in this discourse states, *these cruel, sinful sneerers, vile among men, I repeatedly hurl back into the world, to be born into demonic homes.* This is a retributive view of human psychospiritual nature and of reincarnation. Is it too crude a perspective?

Third, and in opposition to my last question, this discourse makes a vivid point when it says, *Driven by insatiable desires, filled with hypocrisy, conceit and arrogance, ignorantly embracing deluded ideas, these men of vile doctrines stamp through the world.* This describes today's egotistical, poisonous and war mongering leaders who upturn lives and cause misery and pain. May such people legitimately be called demonic?

A final question, many people are undoubtedly born into hellish conditions, and live miserable existences. What is the ultimate cause of this? Choice? Innate nature? Chance? Karma? Does anything beneficial come out of living a traumatic life? The views proposed in this discourse provide readers with concepts to stimulate deep analysis.

DISCOURSE SEVENTEEN

My reading of this discourse is that it was written in response to the proceeding discourse. This is seen in the question with which the discourse begins: *Krishna, those men who cast the sacred texts aside, yet still worship with faith, what is their state? Do they act from sattva, rajas or tamas?* This question shifts the discussion away from the division of people into divine and demonic and back to the concept of the three gunas. Demonic nature is characterised in verse 6 as opposed to sattvic qualities, but that is the only reference to demonic in the discouse. The notion of *divine* presented in the previous discourse is replaced by the guna's sattvic strand.

This discourse is divided into two parts. The first part, which concludes at verse 22, analyses faith, diet, sacrifice, austerity and charity according to the division of the three gunas. It provides a more subtle analysis of human psychological traits and behaviour than the previous discouse. The second part comments on "Om Sat Tat" as a sacred phrase.

Part one is straight forward, presenting a view of how the three gunas manifest in the human psychospiritual domain. Verse 3 interestingly states: *Man's faith conforms to his inner nature. Man is made of faith; whatever the quality of his faith, that is what he becomes.* This verse begins by stating that the quality of our faith conforms to our inner nature, but ends by asserting that our faith shapes our inner nature. Logically, this is a circular argument. But in terms of our psychospiritual nature, it is an insightful comment, arguing for what we today call a feedback loop.

The world is full of feedback loops. An example of an emotional feedback loop is the way people become depressed, and feed that depression by reducing their emotional stimulus, eating in an unhealthy manner, and falling into passivity. These behaviours depress their biological system and spiral them downward into greater depression. In the context of faith, if we find the teaching we receive feeds us inwardly, we are encouraged and want more. If that teaching feeds us positively, we grow. Conversely, if that input feeds us negatively, we inwardly contract.

A number of verses suggest that the writer of this discourse came from brahmanic circles. In verse 14 homage to brahmans is considered to be on a par with homage to the gods, gurus and the wise, while verse 23 states that brahmans were created at the same time as sacrifice and the *Vedas*. The reference in this discourse to reciting sacred texts and to respecting religious authority evokes the world of temple worship, in contrast to the earlier discourses, which celebrate the lone seeker who ignores sacred texts and retreats to the forest to meditate on atman. This shift in perspective and practice reflects the *Bhagavad Gita's* inclusiveness, that it reflects the outlook and practices of all Indian traditions. The inclusiveness extends beyond Vedanta: the division of austerity into body, speech and thought will resonate with worshippers brought up in Zoroastrian, Jewish, Christian and Islamic traditions, as will the comment on differing levels of charity that follow.

The discourse ends with an affirmation of *Om Sat Tat* as the sacred name of Brahman. On the cosmic level, *Om* may be interpreted as referring to Brahman as the transcendent Absolute, *Sat* as referring to Brahman's manifestation as all that exists, and *Tat* as referring to Brahman's manifestation as everlasting, good and true. On the personal level of inward spiritual effort, *Om Sat Tat* can be translated as "You are that". On this level, *Om* may be interpreted as the experience of one's own inner spiritual vibration, *Tat* as the experience of the spiritual essence of all that which is, and *Sat* as this experience being filled with inner truth and light.

DISCOURSE EIGHTEEN

The *Bhagavad Gita's* final discourse reads as a response to the previous two discourses. While it, too, possibly emanated from brahmanic circles, it offers a deeper analysis than the previous two discourses, and returns the poem to the key concepts of obtaining inner knowledge and spiritualising action presented in the earliest discourses. It functions to wrap up the story the the *Bhagavad Gita's* key concepts. Most significantly, it offers guidance on how to apply the *Bhagavad Gita's* teachings in everyday life. Given the content of the discourse, the writer's daily life likely revolved around the brahmanic duties of sacrifice, austerity and charity, which were also central to the previous discourse. Nonetheless, the statements made here regarding action and work apply in all contexts, not just in relation to religious ritual.

The discourse begins with a question from Arjuna. This time the question is with respect to renunciation of action, which gives the discourse its title, *The Yoga of Liberation through Renunciation*. The discourse consists of six parts. The first part discusses the nature of renunciation. The second part begins at verse 12, with the division of action into various contributing factors, which are then analysed according to the gunas. From verse 41 the third part discusses castes in relation to action. Part four starts at verse 50 and recaps what has been stated in previous discourses regarding how a seeker may achieve experiential knowledge of Brahman. Included in this part is a reminder to Arjuna that he needs to fulfil his prescribed duty—in his case, as a warrior—in order to achieve his spiritual destiny. Part five, beginning at verse 64, re-emphasises Krishna's secret teaching, which is surrender to him as a form of Brahman. From verse 72 the final part wraps up the story.

The first part examines two positions in relation to the practice of renunciation: sanyasa and tyaga. The followers of both paths practice renunciation. The difference between them is that sanyasis consider renunciation should be performed while carrying out the action. This is done by purifying intention and by being non-attached while engaged in action. In contrast, tyagis argued that it is rather the results of the action that should be renounced and abandoned. In the earlier discourses on action, both aspects are emphasised equally. But the intricacies of this practice must have been analysed at length over the centuries following the introduction of the practice of karmayoga, and various groups ended up emphasising different aspects of its practice. As the writer observes in verse 3, *Some thinkers proclaim all action is soiled, concluding action should be abandoned; others argue acts of sacrifice, charity, and austerity should never be given up*. Presumably, controversy reigned.

The writer of this discourse responds by returning the discussion to the principles and practices of karmayoga proposed in Discourses Two to Five. Beginning in verse 5, the writer proposes that the religious actions of sacrifice, austerity and charity have to be performed. They should not be renounced, because they are part of the worshipper's duty, and their performance helps seekers to purify their inner selves. However, sacrifice, austerity and charity should be approached from the perspective of karmayoga, being performed in a state of non-attachment, without seeking rewards. Verse 10 then makes a statement that applies to all those who perform actions: *Who does not avoid unpleasant action, nor clings to pleasant action, is an undoubting one who correctly practises abandonment*. Equanimity is the key to not becoming caught up in the opposites of pleasant and unpleasant, attraction and aversion. Thus the practice of the renunciation of action involves our inwardly transcending our attachment to the action while still outwardly engaged in it.

How we accomplish this is described from verse 13, which analyses the best way to perform any action. The factors identified as contributing to action include knowledge, action, the doer, intellect, will and happiness. Each is separated into sattvic, rajasa and tamasa levels. As in the preceding discourse, the analysis is somewhat programmatic. Nonetheless, it offers a commonsense application of the gunic concepts, and is non-judgmental in tone.

Part three offers a perspective on the four castes. It eschews the emphasis on brahmans made in the previous discourse. Instead, from verse 41, the writer first identifies the social qualities and value of the castes, then moves on to discuss their spiritual qualities, offering the same analysis for each: that work should become a form of worship, that individuals fulfil their social destiny by carrying out the work that presents itself to them, and that by completing work with a pure attitude, while maintaining an attitude of renunciation, everyone, whatever their caste, may ultimately achieve freedom from action.

The discourse starts to wrap up from verse 50. It begins with a reiteration of previously stated qualities regarding how to achieve perfection and attain oneness with Brahman. This leads, from verse 64, into a recap of the need to abandon one's actions and one's self to Ishvara (Brahman as cosmic Being), Krishna being a symbol of that Being. Finally, Krishna asks Arjuna if his delusion is shattered and so is willing to engage in the battle of life. Arjuna replies, *Devoid now of doubt, I shall do your bidding*. The teaching is complete.

13 Scholars debate how the phrase, *the teachings of sankhya*, should be interpreted. It can't refer to Sankhya philosophy, because the five factors named in the following verse do not accord with Sankhya teaching. Most likely it is meant in a general sense of referring to all systems of spiritual knowledge.

14 The word translated here as *field* is the Sanskrit word, *adhisthana*. It has several meanings. Literally, it means seat or abode. However, adhithana can also refer to what underlies all action. And it can mean that which originates action. So trying to find an equivalent English word is difficult. However, we know that neither purusha nor atman initiate action, so they cannot be what is meant. Further, we know that all action occurs in the realm of prakriti. Therefore, prakriti, out of which all actions ultimately derive, is presumably being referred to. This is also the field referred to in Discourse Thirteen. In order to connect this verse to the earlier discourse, the word *field* has been used here to translate *adhisthana*. But its choice is somewhat arbitrary. Finally, the Sanskrit word,

daiva, has been translated as providence. Depending on the context, *daiva* refers to divine power, the supernatural, destiny or fate. What the writer intends here is to allow for the effect of divine influence on action. Therefore, the inclusive term providence has been selected, given it suggests the allied concepts of destiny and directed intervention.

Glossary

Atman	Literally, self. The spiritual part of each human being.
Bhaktiyoga	The practice of devotion and worship. One of the three principle paths to God-realisation identified in the *Gita*. One who practises this path is a bhakti.
Brahman	God, described as the transcendent, immanent, imperishable Absolute.
Brahman-nirvana	Brahman refers to God as the absolute, while nirvana is the highest form of peace and happiness. Subjectively, it is the state of egolessness, in which the seeker's consciousness is one with Brahman.
Gunas	The gunas permeate the cosmos on all levels. They are sattva, rajas and tamas, the three strands of prakriti. It is due to the gunas interacting that the cosmos originally came into existence.
Ishvara	A term that corresponds to the Western sense of God as the ultimate and transcendent source of all.
Jiva	Literally, creature. Jiva consists of atman plus the senses and mind, along with the accumulation of karmic results which are carried from life to life.
Jnana	Knowledge.
Jnanayoga	The path of knowledge, with a concentration on knowledge of the unmanifest. Meditation is central to its practice. Jnanayogis are called sankhyas.
Karma	Work, which arises out of the interaction of the three gunas. Karma is not used in the *Bhagavad Gita* in our contemporary sense of karma being the result of actions or work.
Karmayoga	The path of action. As a discipline it involves maintaining an inner attitude of non-identification while

	acting, and of being non-attached to the results of any action.
Maya	Illusion. The universe manifested by prakriti that is sustained by the interplay of the three gunas.
Partha	One of Arjuna's numerous alternative names.
Prakriti	Primordial matter, everlasting and indestructible. It manifests the universe through the activity of the gunas, which are its three constituent parts.
Purusha	Primordial, ever-lasting spirit. Identical with Brahman. It is also atman in each being.
Purushottama	Supreme Lord. The term is also used as an epithet for Krishna as Supreme Being.
Rajas	The second and middle one of the three gunas, consisting of energy and passion.
Samadhi	Literally, concentration. In practical terms, samadhi results from the one-pointed focus of awareness when it is directed back towards itself.
Sankhya	One who seeks knowledge through the practice of jnanayoga, with an emphasis on sanyasa.
Sanyasa	Renunciation, generally of worldly concerns, including of family, home, occupation, and so on.
Sanyasi	One who practises sanyasa.
Sattva	The first, and traditionally considered the highest, of the three gunas, consisting of light and knowledge.
Siddhas	Those who possess psychic or spiritual powers.
Tamas	The third and lowest of the three gunas, consisting of darkness and ignorance.
Three worlds	Heaven, earth and underworld.
Vairagya	The attitude of dispassion towards sense objects, in which one instead seeks Brahman.
Vasudeva	Vasudeva was originally a name used by a religious sect to refer to the one God. It later came to be used to refer to Krishna as the one, all-encompassing God. In Indian mythology, Krishna was also the son of Vasudeva, of the Yadava tribe. Vasudeva's sister, Kunti, married Pandu and was Arjuna's mother.

Vedas	The oldest Indian religious writings. Four in number, they consist of texts for rituals and worship, with some parts, the Upanishads, containing mystical teachings. The rituals outlined in the Vedas provide the basis for Indian religious worship.
Yoga	Generally used to denote karmayoga, but may also be used to refer to any practice, philosophy or attitude that takes the seeker towards God-realisation.
Yogi	Generally used to denote one who practises karmayoga. In some chapters of the *Gita* yogis are juxtaposed to sankhyas, who practise jnanayoga. However, yogi may also be used in a general sense to indicate any seeker engaged in practices that lead towards God-realisation.
Yogamaya	Maya means illusion, while here yoga refers to Brahman's manifestation as the universe. From the perspective of atman, Indian spirituality considers that the manifest cosmos hides the reality of Brahman's unmanifest aspect from atman. So the cosmos is considered to be illusory.

To the reader

If you enjoyed this book, please take the time to place a review at the store from which you purchased it. Your support is appreciated, as it will let other readers know your thoughts on the book, and support Keith's continuing work. Information on Keith's other books is available at his author website, www.keithhillauthor.com, and Attar Books, www.attarbooks.com. All books may be purchased from your favourite online store or local bookstore.

This book is one of a series, *Classics of World Mysticism*. Others in the series include:

I Cannot Live Without You
Selected Poetry of Mirabai and Kabir

It's been an eternity since I was hungry for God's pure essence. I Cannot Live Without You reignites a deep passion to see the face of God, even knowing that God has no face. This book will renew your hunger for your sacred flame. —Judith Hoch PhD, author of *Prophecy By the River*

Wild and passionate, Mirabai is India's greatest poet of devotion and love. Married at a young age, after her husband's premature death she dedicated her life to worshipping the flute-playing Krishna. It was a decision that led her parents-in-law to evict her from their home. Mirabai spent the rest of her life travelling from village to village, singing and dancing to celebrate her love of Krishna. The rapturous lyrics she wrote enthralled worshippers then and continue to be sung in India today.

Kabir was a controversial figure. An illiterate weaver, Kabir celebrated both Indian and Muslim spirituality, while criticising each religion's blinkered believers. Yet his straight talking, his wit, and the continued relevance of his insights, ensure his often knotty poems still resonate powerfully for contemporary readers.

Superbly translated into English-language poems that reflect their original imagery and forms, this collection shows why Mirabai and Kabir have enchanted devotees for five centuries. These engaging versions will delight readers new to the work of two of India's greatest mystical poets, and surprise those already familiar with their playful profundity.

Psalms of Exile and Return
A journey in search of inner healing and unity

In a time that seems spiritually dry for so many, this book of psalms is water in the desert. They challenge, terrify, comfort, and call us to a deep humanity. —Allan Jones, Dean Emeritus, Grace Cathedral, San Francisco

In 587 BCE, King Zedekiah of Judah led his people in rebellion against Babylonian rule. Nebuchadnezzar responded mercilessly. His army sacked Jerusalem, destroyed the Temple, and deported thousands to Babylon.

These psalms are written from the perspective of one of those exiles. They express his growing unhappiness with life as a slave, his despairing cries for help to his Lord, and his eventual escape into the wilderness. After much struggle he is reunited with his lost beloved, and together they find their way back to Jerusalem. Inspired by the passionate writings of the ancient Jewish prophets and poets, and in harmony with the Jewish healing tradition of tikkun olam, these poems recount the spiritual journey seekers make as they strive to transcend everyday life, enter their own hurt heart, heal its pain, and experience the wisdom that exists there. It is the story of exiles who, lost and despairing, rediscover themselves in joy.

Interpretations of Desire
Mystical love poems by the Sufi master Ibn 'Arabi

Keith Hill's artful and beautiful renditions will bring Ibn 'Arabi's neglected masterpiece to a new readership. —Nile Green, author of *Sufism: A Global History*

In 1201, Shaykh Muhyiddin Ibn 'Arabi arrived in Mecca. Among the many people who impressed him one drew his attention above all others: Nizám, the daughter of a prominent religious teacher. As Beatrice did for Dante, Nizám soon inspired a sequence of love poems that are Ibn 'Arabi's poetic masterpiece, *Tarjumán al-Aswáq* (*The Interpreter of Desire*).

Muhyiddin Ibn 'Arabi was known as Shaykh al-Akbar (the Greatest Shaykh), a title given him due to his profound knowledge as a mystic, theologian, philosopher and legalist. Scholars are devoting much labour to translating and interpreting Ibn 'Arabi's voluminous prose writings, but his poetry remains little known by Western readers compared with that of his fellow Sufis, Rumi, Attar and Hafiz.

This collection reveals that with his intense feeling, vivid imagery, and the playful way he reworked the conventions of Bedouin desert poetry, Ibn 'Arabi wrote poems that deserve to be placed alongside the best of his illustrious Sufi compatriots. Keith Hill's engaging new English language versions will be welcomed not just by those attracted to Sufi literature, but by all who enjoy enchanting love poetry.

www.ingramcontent.com/pod-product-compliance
Lightning Source LLC
Chambersburg PA
CBHW030439010526
44118CB00011B/701